God's East Anglia

GW00730586

God's East Anglia

P.H. Jeffery

Journeys of discovery among the historic cathedrals, chapels and churches of East Anglia and numerous encounters with saints, kings, soldiers, merchants, housewives, lords and ladies, the high-born and the humble, who have passed this way before.

LEFT – St. Michael's, Stockton, beneath a blanket of snow.

Printed in England by The Burlington Press (Cambridge) Ltd., Foxton, Cambridge.
ISBN 1 870301 04 8

Illustrations

Acknowledgements – the illustration from 'The Bury Bible' (page 80) by courtesy of the Master and Fellows of Corpus Christi College, Cambridge; King's College Chapel, engraving of interior (page 112) by courtesy of the Cambridgeshire Collection. The drawing of St. Edmund at Walpole St. Peter (page 9) is by Jenifer Jeffery. All other illustrations are by the author.

Contents

Introduction

This book is the product of many hundreds of miles of travel. Among my constant companions (camera, notebook and maps) has been a medallion, a gift of many years ago, showing a man with a long stick, up to his knees in water with a child on his left shoulder.

His name is Christopher and we have encountered each other many times. Faded and indistinct, his picture is opposite the door of many old East Anglian churches. He stands there waiting to greet the traveller with the infant Holy Child held high above the waters. When Lound's little church was renovated under the guidance of Ninian Comper just before the First World War, a 20th century version of the saint's portrait was painted on the wall with a car in the background. Later an aeroplane was added to the picture. Of course St. Christopher has not been the only character encountered on my travels around Norfolk, Suffolk, northern Essex and eastern Cambridgeshire, which, for the purpose of this book, constitute East Anglia.

There have been kings and queens; saints, knights and nobles; soldiers, sailors, merchants and ecclesiastics; academics, doctors and lords of manors; dragons and unicorns, angels and uglies – all carved in stone and wood, pictured in coloured glass, painted on walls and screens, or inscribed in brass. And there have been the living; the men and women, stipendiary and lay, who have shown, without exception, patience and kindness.

The choice of which churches to include is personal and, in part at least, was dictated by geography. This is not a guide; many of the buildings mentioned have their own offering, ranging from glossy coloured productions to a sheet run off by a duplicator. For those seeking more expert and detailed guidance there are Sir Nikolaus Pevsner's series 'The Buildings of England' or (for Norfolk and Suffolk) the books by H. Munro Cautley.

Each church, cathedral and chapel has its own unique and fascinating story, told by its fabric, fittings, memorials and situation. Once you have 'cracked the code' of architectural styles the evolutionary tale is usually revealed (hence the glossary of the more commonly encountered terms elsewhere in this book). But churches were built by human hands and that is why many references are made to the cautionary, tragic or plainly pompous epitaphs and memorials of the men and women who sought an earthly immortality.

For centuries East Anglia's churches have been essential and integral features of the landscape – who would remember Ely without its cathedral or Blythburgh without its church? What would Little Walsingham have been but for its shrine or Bury St. Edmunds without its abbey? These hundreds of buildings, be they grand medieval structures like Long Melford, Thaxted and Salle; bright and delightful little gems like Gipping and Shelton; or rustic and architecturally artisan (but thoroughly picturesque) like Cranwich, Edingthorpe and Harleston, are a rich and priceless legacy.

East Anglia's castles (those symbols of earthly might) are, for the most part, ruinous shells or prisons become museums. The major noble houses, so much younger in years than our churches, are often mere echoes of a vanished past presented with all the dull lack of imagination which only corporate custodians could conceive. Our churches, in the majority of cases, are neither lifeless though you may find them silent, nor abandoned though you might find yourself without mortal companionship. They are still used for their original purpose – the worship of God.

Sadly not all East Anglian churches are always open to the casual visitor; some, the victims of vandalism, theft or profanity, have closed their doors on the world (but the key-holder is usually named in the porch). Others accept such acts as the hazards of indisciplined days and refuse to be intimidated. Long may they do so. Vandalism and theft from churches are not modern phenomena, but their profusion is.

To all those, like the husband and wife cleaning at Doddington, the ladies at Salle, the bee-keeping warden at Horham, the stewards at Southwold, the numerous churchyard grass-cutters and many others who made the visits more pleasurable go my thanks.

RIGHT – thatching at St. Botolph's, North Cove.

Missionaries, Saints and Martyrs of East Anglia

When, how or by whom the Christian message first came to East Anglia is unknown. The Roman Legions invaded Britain in 43 AD, marched on Colchester, capital of the Catuvellauni, and then began the subjugation of southern Britain. They extinguished the brutal Druidic cult of Celtic Britain and introduced their own gods – Mars, Jupiter, Venus and others of Classical mythology. At Colchester they built a temple to their deified Emperor Claudius, and later the cult of the Persian god, Mithras, became popular.

Although subjected to severe persecution, Christianity spread throughout the Roman empire. In the third century, Alban, a pagan who had given shelter to a Christian priest, suffered martyrdom at Verulamium (St. Albans) for his conversion. By the fourth century Christianity was firmly rooted with the British Church having its own bishops. Numerous Romano-British artefacts have been discovered bearing the symbols Chi-Rho (Christos) and alpha-omega (Revelations 1.8 'I am Alpha and Omega, the beginning and the ending, saith the Lord').

The Roman administration of Britain collapsed in the early fifth century and a new paganism was established by the invading Anglo-Saxons who worshipped Thunor, the god of thunder, and Woden, the lord of battles. The conversion of the heathen Anglo-Saxon kingdoms of eastern England was achieved during the 7th century under the leadership of men like Felix, Cedd, Fursey and Botolph who were encouraged by the Christian kings of East Anglia and Essex. Redwald, the most powerful of the East Anglian dynasty, had embraced Christianity in a half-hearted manner, keeping an altar to his ancestral gods alongside one for the 'new' religion. His son and successor, Earpwald, was a genuine convert but was assassinated in 627 when his throne was usurped and the kingdom lapsed into a brief period of paganism.

Sigebert became king of East Anglia (a realm covering Norfolk, Suffolk and parts of Cambridgeshire) in 630. He was a fervent Christian and supported the mission of the Burgundian, Felix, who established a centre at Dunwich (it is now thought that Felix's 'Dommoc' may have been the submerged Roman shore fort near Felix-

stowe). Felix died in 647 and was buried at Soham where he had formed a monastery, and his relics were later removed to Ramsey Abbey. Sigebert also fostered the founding of a monastery within the walls of the Roman fort at Burgh Castle which had been built in the third century to protect the coast from Saxon pirates. Its leaders were the Irish brother monks Fursey and Foillan.

King Sigebert abdicated his throne and became a monk himself, establishing a monastic house at Bury St. Edmunds. But they were troubled times; on the realm's western border near Newmarket was the pagan kingdom of Mercia. Led by Penda, the Mercians invaded East Anglia; Sigebert was obliged to lead his countrymen into battle although he refused to wield anything but a stick, and he was killed. Anna ruled until 654 when he was slain by another army of invading Mercians led by Penda. After the battle of Bulcamp, Anna's body and that of his son, Jurmin, who was later revered as a saint, were buried at Blythburgh.

Anna's other offspring achieved greater fame. Ethelburga and her step-sister Saethrith became nuns and abbesses in France; Etheldreda (St. Audrey, whose name was corrupted to give 'tawdry' from the poor quality goods sold at medieval fairs) founded an abbey at Ely. She was followed as abbess by her sister Sexburga, whose daughters also became abbesses.

In the Kingdom of the East Saxons, ruled by another Sigebert, it was Cedd, a monk of Lindisfarne, who led the evangelising mission from monasteries he had formed at Tilbury and the old Roman shore fort at Bradwell-on-Sea. Only traces remain of the fort but the saint's 7th century church still stands above the marshes of the Blackwater. In 654, while Cedd was building his church at Bradwell, Botolph was establishing a monastery at Iken near the River Alde. At Chich, near the estuary of the Colne, Osith, the wife of another East Saxon king, the apostate Sighere, established a convent.

Other figures from the 7th and 8th centuries who were venerated as saints during the medieval period were Guthlac, the hermit of Crowland, his disciples Bettelin and Cissa, his sister Pega, and Ovin and Huna, two companions of Etheldreda at Ely. Ethelbert, an East Anglian king murdered in 794, was revered as a Christian martyr but the most famous of the royal East Anglian saints of the Saxon period was King Edmund who was martyred by Danish invaders in 869. The young king, who refused to save his life by becoming the invaders' vassal and denying his faith, was killed by archers and his body decapitated. Numerous legends arose concerning Edmund – his head, it was claimed, was guarded by a wolf, and that he made a ghostly appearance to slay Sweyn Forkbeard when the Dane threatened to burn the monastery which housed Edmund's shrine. Carvings of the saint's head being watched over by a wolf are at Hadleigh and Walpole St. Peter. He also appears on several medieval screens (Barton Turf, Ludham and others) and in wall paintings as at Fritton, Thornham Parva and Lakenheath.

The Danes who martyred Edmund expunged monastic Christianity from East Anglia. Monasteries were looted and destroyed, more names such as abbot Hedda of Peterborough and the hermits of Thorney were added to the list of Christian martyrs, and a century elapsed before monasticism was revived.

Walstan of Bawburgh and Wendreda of March attracted local devotional cults as did Godric, the Norfolk-born hermit who retired to Northumbria. The alleged kinsmen of Edmund, Edwold, who lived on bread and water in Dorset, and Fremund, were subjects of minor, localised approbation as was Blida of Martham, who was said to have been Walstan's mother.

Two cults of boys, the supposed victims of Jewish ritual murder, emerged in the 12th century. The first, of William of Norwich, began in 1144 and his pictures are on screens at Loddon, Eye and Worstead. In 1181 Suffolk had a rival in Robert of Bury St. Edmunds (Lincoln followed in 1255 with its own 'Little Saint Hugh'). Many of these saints were depicted in medieval Church art with their personal symbols – Edmund holding an arrow, Walstan with a scythe, Withburga accompanied by a doe.

The Apostles, Biblical saints, and martyrs of the early Church were favourite subjects for artists in the medieval period when they were used pictorially in glass and paint to instruct and inspire largely illiterate congregations. Fortunately, East Anglia still has many examples of pre-Reformation screen and wall paintings although some have been cruelly treated. Notable examples of screen paintings are at Worstead, Ranworth, Southwold, Westhall and Kersey. Murals were one of the earliest forms of decoration and St. Christopher was a popular figure. St. George killing a dragon, Biblical

ABOVE – a carving of the wolf guarding the crowned head of the martyred St. Edmund at Walpole St. Peter.

scenes, the cautionary tale of the Three Living and Three Dead, the Seven Works of Mercy and the Last Judgement or Doom were other recurrent themes. Among examples are those at Copford, North Cove, Wissington, Wickhampton, Wenhaston and Fritton. Medieval church glass suffered terribly at the hands of William Dowsing and other Puritan iconoclasts so that what remains is often fragmentary. King's College Chapel, Cambridge, has an unmatched series of windows from the early 16th century and Long Melford has Suffolk's finest collection.

Foreign saints and martyrs, some of doubtful or even invented existence, gained popular appeal and their protection or assistance was invoked in a variety of circumstances. Agatha, it was believed, protected against fire; Leonard was the protector of prisoners; Apollonia assisted when toothache occurred; Erasmus, a patron of mariners, also helped with stomach troubles; and Uncumber (Wilgefortis) could rid a wife of an unwanted spouse. Kings are to be found on some surviving screens. Edward the Confessor, Henry VI and Olaf of Norway all appear at Barton Turf near that church's wonderfully colourful array of angels.

The 15th and 16th centuries added hundreds more

names to the roll of Christian martyrs. Men and women, rich and poor, scholars and labourers were imprisoned, tortured and executed during years of religious persecution. Followers of John Wyclif were burned as heretics in the Lollard's Pit at Norwich where Thomas Bilney was executed. Sir Thomas More and Bishop John Fisher were notable victims of the tyranny of Henry VIII. Many more died during the Marian repression; Thomas Cranmer, Nicholas Ridley and Hugh Latimer, the Oxford Martyrs burned in 1556, had been educated at Cambridge where John Hullier the parish priest of Babraham was burned on Jesus Green. Rowland Taylor of Hadleigh died on Aldham Common; his curate, Richard Yeoman, was burned at Norwich and East Bergholt priest, Robert Samuel, was executed at Ipswich. Among others who died for their beliefs were a Lynn merchant, a Laxfield shoemaker, an apothecary from Colchester, a labourer from Framsden and a Mendlesham weaver. Jesuits Robert Southwell and Henry Walpole, both born in Norfolk and executed in Elizabeth's reign, were among numerous Roman Catholics put to death.

The dissolution of the monasteries resulted in the destruction of some of East Anglia's finest ecclesiastical buildings. Peterborough's abbey church was saved by being reconstituted as a cathedral. In some instances conversion to parochial use saved priory buildings as at Binham, Wymondham and Little Dunmow; at Cambridge, Magdalene and Emmanuel Colleges were founded in monastic buildings and Sidney Sussex was built on the site of the Greyfriars' house. Earlier, Jesus College had been formed in 1496 in a suppressed nunnery and St. John's in a monastic hospital.

Following the Norman Conquest the powerful Benedictine abbeys of eastern England (Bury St. Edmunds, St. Benet's Hulme, Ely, Crowland and others) were supplemented by numerous smaller monastic establishments controlled by other orders. The Norman barons were active in founding priories – Binham, Bromholm, Castle Acre, Thetford, Old Buckenham and Colchester were early examples – and monasticism expanded rapidly.

Earliest of the new monastic orders which were formed as a result of opinion that many Benedictine monasteries had become too rich and worldly were the Cluniacs centred on the French abbey of Cluny. William de Warenne established the first Cluniac priory in England at Lewes and he founded another near his Norfolk stronghold at Castle Acre.

The Cistercians or White Monks originated at Cîteaux and were a brotherhood of strict regime who built their monasteries in remote areas. Their finest buildings are Fountains and Rievaulx abbeys in North Yorkshire. At the Conquest East Anglia was the most populous region of the kingdom so the Cistercians built few houses in the area – at Sibton, Tilty and Little Coggeshall and a nunnery near Narborough. Most numerous were the Augustinians (the Austin or Black Canons) who served, worked and preached in their local communities. Among their many houses were North Creake, Weybourne, Little Walsingham, Ixworth, Wicken, Little Dunmow and St. Osyth. Smaller orders were the Premonstratensians or White Canons with a few abbeys which included Langley and Leiston, and the English Gilbertine order who occupied Fordham abbey.

In the 13th century various orders of friars made their appearance in England. These were brotherhoods following strict rules of poverty and prayer laid down by their founders, men like the Spaniard, Dominic, and Francis of Assisi. The leading orders of friars, Dominicans (Black Friars), Franciscans (Grey Friars), Carmelites (White Friars), and Austin Friars established houses in the major towns such as Norwich, Ipswich, Thetford, Cambridge, Great Yarmouth and Lynn.

By the early 16th century some, but not all, monasteries had fallen to a level well below that of their founders' intention. They provided a modicum of charity and medical care for the poor and aged which was lost when they were suppressed by Henry VIII. Buildings and estates passed to the Crown and were later sold to the rich, some being converted into country houses; others like St. Edmund's Abbey were demolished.

LEFT – St. Mary's, Hadleigh, and Deanery Tower.

The Parish Church – a familiar vision in the English landscape

The English parish church, usually the most ancient building in its locality, is an historic and cherished institution although, sometimes, its services may be sparsely attended. As the oldest Christian centres of their communities, parish churches have been immensely important in the development of English society and they are prime contributors to the history of architecture, some dating from the Norman period, some from the late Anglo-Saxon age.

For a thousand years parish churches have been familiar landmarks in the English countryside. Most of them, apart from Victorian restoration, renovation and repair, and a change of roof-covering from thatch to slate or tiles, are essentially the same as they were 500 years ago. Some of early foundation have remained small with only chancel, nave and tower while others have evolved into huge buildings with aisles and transepts. In some Anglo-Saxon or Norman work is at their core; others incorporate little or nothing from the churches they replaced.

When the Norman conquerors claimed the kingdom as the spoils of war, England had an effective and efficient structure of government. The realm was divided into counties which were sub-divided into smaller administrative districts known as hundreds. Most parishes had a church and Norwich, the largest town in the region with around 7,000 people, had 20 churches. The country churches of late Anglo-Saxon England were usually small wooden structures, some with a flint-faced circular tower which was probably used as refuge and look-out point (a chronicler tells how a Balsham man survived a Danish massacre by defending himself in the church tower). The great majority of surviving round church towers are in Norfolk and Suffolk – 160 between them – notably near the coast or rivers which were highways for piratical raids.

Some of the wooden churches of Anglo-Saxon East Anglia, built with split log walls like those of the mid-9th century walls at Greensted-juxta-Ongar, occupied sites of early Christian and pagan worship. In 601 Pope Gregory instructed Augustine to cleanse the pagan temples with holy water, destroy their idols and adapt the buildings for Christian rites with altars and holy relics. Eastern England's oldest Christian building is St. Cedd's church at Bradwell-on-Sea. Other surviving work of Anglo-Saxon church-builders includes that at St. Benet's, Cambridge, Debenham, Strethall and Hadstock and the ruined minster at North Elmham.

The Normans injected a new and energetic impetus into English church building. Their work is characterised by the semi-circular arch as in the massive arcades of Ely and Norwich cathedrals and Wymondham; sturdy square towers as at South Lopham and Bury St. Edmunds, and in the doorways with dog tooth and zig-zag decoration of many smaller parish churches such as Hales, Wissington, Kirtling, Great Bradley and Wissett. Increased economic activity and prosperity, as well as a rapid expansion of the population, led to a new burst of church building and the adoption of the more graceful, lighter and taller styles of construction of the Early English and Decorated periods. The round Norman arch gave way to the pointed arch above slender columns decorated with delicately carved foliage. Narrow lancets, sometimes grouped in threes, evolved into wide windows with curving tracery and the austere, dim Norman interiors became brighter and bigger with aisles and extended naves and chancels. West Walton is an outstanding example of 13th century craftsmanship. The elaboration of the Decorated style came to an abrupt end with the Black Death of 1349 when between a third and a half of the population died.

In the aftermath of the plague came social change which loosened feudal bonds and animated religious life with new fervour and devotion. The 14th and 15th centuries brought a huge upsurge in church building and rebuilding. East Anglia's cloth manufacturing gave many workers a new affluence and made some merchants very rich. The wealth of these men and their trade guilds is reflected in the magnificent East Anglian 'wool' churches such as Lavenham, Long Melford and Worstead. Other examples of ambitiously planned reconstruction and enlargement are Salle, Thaxted, which benefited from the town's cutlery trade, and the coastal port churches at Brightlingsea, Southwold, and Cley.

RIGHT – St. Peter and naked souls from Wenhaston's Doom.

Walberswick and Covehithe built big new churches during their days of maritime prosperity but they fell into ruin when fortune deserted the townships. Notable smaller Perpendicular churches are at Shelton, Denston and the Tyrell chapel at Gipping.

In the areas where wealthy nobles, clothiers and merchants were generous patrons, the parish churches of the century before the Reformation became colourful and luxuriously furnished buildings. Religion was practiced with elaborate pageantry and ceremony – processions of banners, the rich vestments of the clergy and the colour of stained glass, paintings and images imbued community worship with ceremonial pomp, pageantry and theatrical splendour. The Perpendicular architectural style dominated during the three centuries after the Black Death and it is the commonest feature of ecclesiastical buildings. Wide windows flooded the interiors with light; carvings in wood and stone proliferated inside and out; and new, majestic hammerbeam roofs, some carved with figures of angels and saints as at March, Knapton, Woolpit and Needham Market, were lit by clerestory windows. Wealthy families and guilds established chantry chapels where regular prayer was offered for the well-being of the patrons' souls; tomb art developed from the stiff medieval figures carved in stone, wood and brass via kneeling and reposing effigies in Tudor armour and gowns, to the 18th century statues of worthies reclining in cushioned opulence.

Among the oldest items of sacramental furniture still preserved in churches are the fonts which, in East Anglia, range from weighty, square Norman pieces to the stepped Seven Sacrament fonts such as those at Badingham, Cratfield, Laxfield, Seething and Sloley. The Norman fonts at Fincham and Burnham Deepdale are famous for their figure carvings, the latter bearing a calendar of rural activities such as digging, weeding, harvesting and a Christmas feast. Towering font-covers and canopies gave medieval carpenters the opportunity to display skill and ingenuity and remarkable examples survive at Ufford, Castle Acre and Trunch. Timber benches with ends and arm rests embellished by intricately carved poppy heads and human and saintly figures appeared in the 15th century. Previously seating had been uncommon and consisted of stone benches along the walls. Fine examples of benches with elaborate decoration are at Fressingfield, Ufford, Wiggenhall St. Germans and Wiggenhall St. Mary the Virgin.

Upon a pew built by Steven Crosbee at Little Barningham in 1640 'for couples joyned in wedlocke' stands the disconcerting figure of a shrouded skeleton with hour glass and scythe.

For centuries the church was the grandest, most durable and sometimes the only stone-built building in its parish. A particularly East Anglian feature of the region's late medieval churches is the flushwork external decoration of patterns, symbols and words in carved stone and flint. In the 15th century many grand porches were added, some of two storeys with the upper room used variously as lady chapel, treasury or, as at Mendlesham, the parish armoury. The importance of porches as a place of business is reflected by the verse at Eye--

Seale not to soone lest thou repente to late,
Yet helpe thy frend, but hinder not thy state.
If ought thou lende or borrow, truly pay,
Ne give, ne take advantage, though thou may,
Let conscience be thy guide, so helpe thy frend,
With loving peace and concord make thy end.

The accumulating richness and splendour of decoration and furnishing in stone, wood, glass and textile was ended in the 16th century. Proximity to and regular contact with the Continent meant East Anglia was heavily influenced by new ideas. The Dutch scholar Erasmus, who taught and fostered the 'New Learning' at Cambridge, poured scorn on the claims of shrines and relics such as those at Little Walsingham and Canterbury. With publication of the Bible in English and its unstoppable importation, the movement for reform became irresistible. The banning of religious guilds, chantries and the eventual dissolution of the monasteries heralded the full blast of the Reformation.

Erasmus had hoped that reform, by the consent and co-operation of all sections of Christendom, would usher in a golden age; instead, in England and northern Europe, the Reformation meant a revolution in Christian thought and ritual which brought the destruction of much which, while intrinsically beautiful, was considered idolatrous. The destruction of treasures and fittings was greatest in England's churches during the reign of the boy-king, Edward VI, and was later compounded by the zeal of Puritans and Cromwell's soldiery. The reformers' wrath was directed principally at images, shrines, and roods. Some glass was smashed but much was left because of the cost of its replacement with clear panes. Plenty remained for William Dowsing to destroy in 1643. Puritanical outrage at anything smacking of superstition resulted in further bouts of mutilation and destruction when brasses were torn up, images defaced, figures on the almost exclusively East Anglian Seven Sacrament fonts were mutilated, and altar slabs smashed or used for paving, as at Cranwich and Great Bircham. Wall paintings were hidden beneath coats of whitewash and even 'weepers' on tombs were decapitated.

Pulpits achieved a new status as preaching gained in importance, as shown in Yaxley church which has a rare sexton's wheel. The pulpit, dated 1635, is carved with the churchwardens' initials and a text from 1 Corinthians – 'Necessite is laid upon me yea woe is me if I preach not the gospel'. Some pulpits of pre-Reformation date with wine glass contours remain, some with picture panels of the Latin Doctors (Ss. Ambrose, Augustine, Gregory and Jerome) as at Burnham Norton.

A much venerated feature of the medieval church which was destroyed during the mid-16th century was the rood group of Christ crucified, the Virgin Mary and St. John. The rood screen separated chancel and nave, and stairs (now usually blocked) gave access to the rood loft above which was placed the rood group. The destruction of roods and rood lofts was markedly thorough but many churches, particularly in Norfolk, retain screens although often in a much reduced form.

Screen pictures of saints, kings and martyrs vary in merit and many have been defaced. Attleborough's screen with surviving loft carrying the arms of 24 bishoprics across the nave and aisles, and that with reconstructed loft and rood at Eye show how rich in colour and carving, and dominating in character they were. Among the region's notable screens is the angel host at Barton Turf and those at Ranworth, Southwold, Worstead, Ludham and Loddon which has a rare picture of William of Norwich. At Fritton, Norfolk, where there are wall paintings of St. Christopher and St. George, the kneeling figure of the donor of the screen, John Bacon, is shown with his wife and children.

In the 17th and 18th century dissenting sects built their places of worship. At Walpole a house was converted into a chapel during the Civil War and later enlarged with three mast-like timber columns supporting the roof. Surrounding the pulpit are benches and galleries of scrubbed wood. Also built during the 17th century were Norwich Old Meeting House, the Unitarian Meeting House at Ipswich and the tiny, simply furnished 'puritan' chapel-of-ease at Guyhirn. Nonconformity flourished in the late 18th and 19th centuries with the rise of Methodism and many East Anglian towns and villages soon had a Chapel Lane or Chapel Street leading to a new place of worship.

After the high passions of the Reformation and Civil War periods the Anglican Church entered a period of torpidity, the Norwich Diocese being dubbed 'the Dead See'. Resentment at the payment of tithes, benefices without resident priests, and the opinion that the parson was the squire's ally in a strictly stratified society caused Anglicanism to be held in wide disrepute. Many churches and cathedrals fell into decay and disrepair until they were rescued by Victorian restoration. The repairs and renovations of the 19th century were often destructive, insensitive and undiscriminating. Wenhaston's doom, which had been painted on a wooden board, was thrown out during restoration but was fortunately revealed by an overnight shower of rain.

New parish churches were built in the Georgian period and one example, built in Classical style to harmonise with its neighbouring Hall, is the redundant church at Gunton. Hierarchical seating was a prominent though not new feature of Georgian Anglicanism with the squire's family pew occupying a prominent position, see Kedington and Thurning. During Victorian restoration many old box pews were replaced but many examples of Stuart seating survive, as well as fine woodwork in the form of three-decker pulpits as at Worlingworth, Warham St. Mary, Kedington and Wilby, Norfolk. Older woodwork can be found in the form of church chests, some of them iron-bound with a multiplicity of locks.

Assisted by government grants, charitable trusts, local appeals and donations, many of East Anglia's churches are now in good repair; others face tremendous problems. For enthusiast, casual visitor or parishioner they may be treasures of history, curiosities or a 'taken for granted' familiar feature of town or village. Whether cathedral, church or chapel, each is a part of God's East Anglia.

'Nerefear soe many washings'

Surely our Sinns were tinctured in graine,
May we not say, the labour was in vaine;
Soe many Washings, still the Spotts remaine.

Marshland – the low, frequently-flooded land between the Nene and Great Ouse – was a poor, perilous, and sparsely populated place when the Normans came; only half a dozen families lived at Walpole then. In the century before the Black Death the salt marshes were drained to graze sheep; new, fast-growing communities formed and, to mark their enterprising advance and prosperity, they built some superb churches.

The threat of flood, however, was constant and, as a board in West Walton church tells, the land had to endure 'many Washings' when, as in 1613, *the Sea broke in and overflowed all Marshland to the grate danger of Mens lives, and loss of goods.* The church tower at Terrington St. Clement was a haven during those November floods (which swept away Parson Drove's chancel) and was so again in 1671, boats from King's Lynn bringing food to the stranded inhabitants. In 1735 at Clenchwarton it was rector's son, Francis Forster, who *when the terrible Inundation threatning the destruction of this whole Level, he with unshaken resolution when all around him droop'd under their Misery, opposed the Flood, repaired the broken Ramparts and sav'd the Land from fatal ruin with which the next assault must have overwhelm'd it. But alass! how short his enjoyment of his rescu'd Country!*

Godric, in turn pedlar, sea captain, pilgrim, hermit and saint, was a teenage son to one of Walpole's few families when the Normans recorded its poor worth. Now there are four distinct Walpole settlements and, at Walpole St. Peter, a Bustards Lane is a reminder of the great birds that once flew over the marshes. The large parish church incorporates in its tower the only surviving part of its forebear which was swept away by the sea in 1337. Over the next hundred years a new and grander church was built up to the boundary of God's Acre so a processional passage (known as the bolt hole) passes beneath the rising floor of the chancel.

In the porch is an old pair of Marshland pattens with a notice requesting their removal from feet before entry.

LEFT – the church at Walpole St. Peter.

Nave and aisle seating is concealed by a Stuart screen which stretches from wall to wall across flagstones and ledgers and there is much other woodwork of that period – pulpit, benches, ringers' gallery, font cover and a box thrice carved with the words 'Remember the poore 1639'. Amid older carvings in the chancel are arm rests of St. Edmund's crowned head between the paws of a guardian wolf. Walpole St. Peter's list of the old, rare, fine and curious is extensive – roof bosses; gargoyles; pictures of saints on the chancel screen; a huge multi-armed brass chandelier; rocking cradle; a lightweight shelter shaped like a sentry box to keep the parson dry at funerals, and a worn stone figure which legend claims to be the effigy of the giant-killer, Tom Hickathrift.

Closer to the sea is Terrington St. Clement whose large church of Barnack stone makes claim to being Marshland's cathedral. Here a Georgian screen runs across the nave and aisles, the font is crowned by a tall cover which opens to reveal scenes from Christ's life, there is a statue of St. Christopher wading through the water with the Holy Infant on his shoulder and huge, decorated boards painted with the Lord's Prayer and Commandments in 1635. St. Clement's detached tower is only a few feet from the church to the north-west; at West Walton it stands several yards to the south.

West Walton's church and tower were built in the early 13th century and are exemplary masterpieces of the Early English architectural style. The tower has an open arch on each side, arcading and great belfry windows. The porch has blank arcading too, and its entrance, between two great pinnacles, is spanned by a 16th century brick gable. Sculpted foliage adorns the nave arcade piers which have detached shafts of Purbeck marble (although some are now wood). The interior is graceful, simple and spacious – little more than a few chairs, stepped font and an old table tomb occupy the brick and flagstone nave and aisles. Painted patterns as old as the church decorate the clerestory beneath which are emblems of the Tribes of Israel.

A few months after the sea flood of 1613, winter rains caused the rivers to burst their banks and Marshland was *overflowed with the fresh* before the skies cleared with, perhaps, a rainbow. West Walton's flood board ends hopefully too –

Heavens face is clear, though the Bow appeare
Reader nerefear, there is no Arrow neare.

A shameless Norman and Fen adventurers

It is a low, flat land of drains and droves; meres, lodes and cuts; causeways, catchwaters and fens. This is Fenland, a reclaimed terrain of dark-soiled farms, belts of windbreak trees, villages of severely distinctive mould, and a grid of straight tracks and roads whose course is governed by the waterways. Intriguing names reflect the old ways of a unique, once insular, suspicious and mysterious land.

Hoghill, Market way and Oxholme; Monk's lode, Parson's drove and Foulmire fen are some of the names to be discovered around the Ouse in southern Fenland. But the Cambridgeshire fen landscape of today is man-made, the result of 17th and 18th century drainage schemes under the supervision of Dutch engineers like Cornelius Vermuyden. The 'Adventurers' – men who speculated their capital in the schemes – were rewarded with grants of the new-drained farming land and so several areas became known as Adventurers Fen.

Three churches of distinct character and attention, separated by the relics of ancient conflicts, stand along the fen edge north of Cambridge. Cottenham's landmark tower has an ashlar base with yellow and pink Jacobean bricks rising to pineapple-like pinnacles. The tower was rebuilt in brick after the original had toppled in a gale in 1617, destroying the churchyard schoolroom in its fall. Eighty years later the school was rebuilt by Katherin Pepys, a contemporary relative of diarist Samuel Pepys whose family had managed the manor for the abbots of Crowland. Cut into the stone face of the tower are the names of benefactors who paid for the 1617 rebuilding, and, three centuries later, an American President gave towards another restoration of the tower. He was Calvin Coolidge whose antecedent John spent his boyhood in the village at the time the old tower fell and then sailed to a new life in America. Another Cottenham lad was Thomas Tenison who went on to become Archbishop of Canterbury, so emulating William Warham who had been rector in Tudor times. The church, mainly of 15th century date, was severely restored when Victorians removed the gallery.

Rampton's little church, roofed with thatch, slate and tile, and a tower sundial of its own, escaped Victorian

LEFT – All Saints' Church, Cottenham.

discipline, and like Croydon, is an historical and rustic jewel of the Christian past. Much of the church was built before the Black Death with pieces of Saxon stone coffins set in the wall. There are wall paintings including St. Christopher near his riverside hermit cell; an agrarian queenpost roof, Elizabethan pulpit and tester, reeling red brick Georgian porch and an effigy, seven centuries old, of a mail-clad lord of the manor. Close by is Giant's Hill, a fort built to contain the Mandeville outlaws in their fenny lair.

Willingham, another of the fen edge villages given by Saxon thanes to a Fenland abbey, has an older fort – the pre-Roman Belsar's Hill. Its church with 14th century tower and spire and one of the county's finest roofs, has wall paintings, some as old as Rampton's stone knight. There is a bearded St. Christopher bearing the infant Christ, a huge St. George and dragon and a female saint in robe of red and yellow – is she Etheldreda to whose Ely foundation Uva gave the manor a thousand years ago?

For Ely's abbot and monks the Conquest was a time of tumult. Hereward's guerilla war was crushed but Picot, the Norman sheriff, had helped himself to much of the estate, including lands at Cottenham, Rampton, Willingham and Waterbeach. The abbot complained so much about this 'greedy hog' who feared not God nor St. Etheldreda – the shameless Norman boasted that he had never heard of her! – that the king ordered an inquiry. Ely's abbot also lost land at Waterbeach to two of the king's carpenters where, in 1160, an isolated offshoot of the monastery was formed near Car Dyke, a Roman canal linking the Cam and Ouse. The monks' tenure was brief; a decade later the Knights Templars took occupation but following the suppression of that military Order some nuns of the Franciscan Order of St. Clare, who had formed a house near the village church, adapted the Templars' church, hospital and buildings to their own use. The cells of monks and nuns which proliferated in and around the fens at Denny, Swaffham Bulbeck, Fordham, Isleham, Wicken and Lode, like their richer and grander brethren at Ely, Thorney, Crowland and Ramsey, have been swept away. In the 19th century a different style of preacher came to Fenland, men like young Charles Spurgeon, and men and women, boys and girls clad in white were baptismally dipped in river waters.

Westhorpe's Queen and 'Hamlet'

How they must have gawped. Such a gathering of bishops and abbots, knights and high-born ladies at their Duke's moated Suffolk home. It was high summer but the village gossip was not of the fast-approaching harvest but of the death of a beautiful queen who had died so soon after her brother, Henry VIII, had made Ann Boleyn his wife. These important men of Church and State had come to Westhorpe to escort the embalmed royal body to Bury St. Edmunds.

During the slow journey to the Abbey of St. Edmund in July, 1533, an effigy of the dead Mary Tudor, dressed in finest robes and a golden crown, was carried with the coffin. Only five years later the great abbey was marked for destruction and Mary's body was moved to the town's church of St. Mary where her remains lie after 18th century disturbance when locks of golden hair were cut from her head. The Hall where she had died at the age of 38 has gone and Westhorpe's only reminder of the days she spent in quiet retreat with the man she loved is an unpretentious plaque in the parish church.

The building, beside the village's only street, is, like Icklingham's redundant All Saints, one of the best examples of a church free of Victorian renovation. The south door, still with tracery carved before a Tudor wore England's crown, leads down to uncluttered aisles and nave with undulating floors of brick, medieval tiles and stone slabs from which all the brasses have been removed. The core of the church is 14th century with aisles and tower built later at the cost of Dame Elizabeth Elmham whose soldier-husband had prospered in foreign wars.

The nave has a dozen simple benches greying with age and a plain font on brick steps. An aisle chapel has a 14th century screen and in the chancel an effigy of William Barrow in Tudor armour faces his curiously-hatted wives. In the Barrow chapel a lifesize figures lies in less pietous pose – here is Maurice Barrow, who died in 1666, reclining in his nightgown (left) with one hand upon his breast like an old time actor declaiming Hamlet's final speech, *Oh! I die Horatio, the potent poison quite o'er-crows my spirit . . . The rest is silence. (dies).* To ensure that his rest was indeed silent and that his marble

LEFT – the Barrow memorial, Westhorpe.

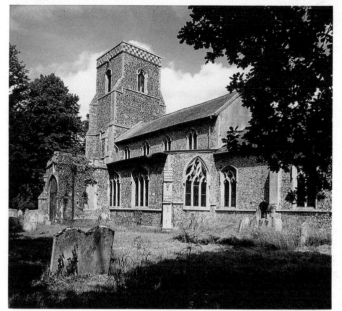

immortality remained inviolate he ordered railings to be put up.

There is no human likeness or Latin eulogy on Richard Elcock's brass. *Pastor of this Congregation, an holy, able and Faithfull Minister of the Gospell of Christ Jesus*, he died in 1630 and in rhyming English we are told –

This Faithful, Learned, Humble Man of God
While in her Earthly tent his Soule Abode
Did to his Flock by Voice and Practise Preach,
His Life Expressing what his Toungue did Teach.
of Grace and Vertue an Unfayned Lover,
of Sin A Zealous, yet Discreet Reprover,
Here Rests his Corps, his Soule in Glory Dwells
His Name Like Pretious Ointment Sweetly Smells.

History does not apply that final epithet to Charles Brandon, Duke of Suffolk. He was not among the mourning throng when his wife, Mary Tudor, was buried in Bury's abbey and he soon took Kate Willoughby, his teenage ward, as his fourth bride. Their two sons went off to study at Cambridge where they died of the seating sickness on the same July day in 1555. Brandon's daughter by Mary married Henry Grey who became Duke of Suffolk and plotted to make his daughter Jane the Queen of England but lost his head instead. The Suffolk dukedom was never revived.

Justice and death near Gallows Hill

Take a minor road from Botesdale, come down from Redgrave's Gallows Hill and in front of you, but for the width of the road, is the 'island' of Norfolk. On the left the Little Ouse begins its westward journey to Thetford and The Wash; on your right the Waveney trickles eastward to grow wide in its search for the sea. Here is the only place (except for bridges) where you can walk into Norfolk and not get your feet wet.

Ahead is the massive tower of South Lopham church – proud, strong and confident like the ruthless Norman family of conquerors who built it. William Bigod was the royal favourite whose wealth enabled this monument to Norman piety and self-esteem to be added to an older Saxon house of worship. Ill-fated William Bigod ended up getting more than his feet wet – he went down with the heir to England's throne in the White Ship disaster in the Channel in 1120. The drunkard crew ran the vessel onto rocks and drowned with their noble passengers – only a French butcher survived – so paying for their murderous folly which would earn the curses of an unhappy land. Treacherous brother Hugh claimed the Bigod estates and helped Stephen of Blois grab the English crown for which he was made Earl of Norfolk. When broken-hearted Henry I quitted hold of his earthly kingdom there was a tribe of royal bastards but no male heir and the anarchy of Stephen's civil wars ensued to which Hugh Bigod contributed his share of turncoat politics. According to The Anglo-Saxon Chronicle, it was a time when Christ and his saints were sleeping.

A huge copper beech, its leaves aglow in summer like the embers of a winter log fire, stands sentry by the churchyard gate. Amid ranks of headstones are cherry and oak, holly and juniper, apple and pine, cedar and silver birch. Above all rises the tower, five storeys tall, four of them embellished with sturdy Norman arches, plus decorated battlements of the 15th century. In the years after the Black Death the chancel was built and the pre-Conquest nave refashioned, retaining a small, round, deep-splayed Saxon window. Inside are benches with carved ends and an ancient chest, eight feet long, cut from a single block of oak.

In the cherished churchyard epitaph hunters find no waist-high nettles or grass to hinder their search. No need to search at all; the headstones and their words have been catalogued by the village Women's Institute – would that every parish was as meticulous in recording its fast-fading history. So it is easy to find South Lopham's versions of the familiar *Farewell vain world. . .* For two old men who died before Victoria was queen and who knew the ache of earthly toil, the adieus end with a tinge of bitter thankfulness *in the grave no work is to be done*. Here, too, are human tragedies: a teenage boy killed in a shooting accident and an elderly woman who died when a paraffin lamp exploded. Beside the boy lies Thomas Cox who *performed a most heroic act in endeavouring to prevent a dynamite explosion at the Houses of Parliament.*

Across the fields to the westward is Bressingham's church. Much rebuilt when Henry VIII was king, its benches are carved with nightmarish creatures and defaced and beheaded figures. At Fersfield is a piece of much older and rarer woodwork – the effigy of 13th century knight, Sir Robert de Bois. Southward from Lopham's Norman tower, on the Suffolk side of the boundary rivers where the farm fields climb out of the Waveney valley, is Redgrave's large and lonely church almost a mile from its village.

Here, unlike Fersfield's recessed wooden knight, the cold, stone memorials are vaunting and proud. Juxtaposed with plain 'Free' benches is the dour-faced armoured effigy of Sir Nicholas Bacon, son of Elizabeth's Keeper of the Great Seal, and beside him lies his no less ill-humoured wife, Anne Butts. Her long-lived mother who *seaven fayer yeares she spent in wedlock sage; and since that merry age sixty one yeares she lived a widdowe sage* is shown with severe face on a fine chancel brass. A wall tablet to Elizabeth, wife of Sir Edmund Bacon, tells that she was a *prudent governess of her family* and that *she had 6 sons and 10 daughters four of which only and no son lived to the state of marriage*. Hatchments abound in the nave and watching over all in the chancel, seated bewigged and gowned in high juridical splendour between the statues of Justice and Vigilance, is the figure of Sir John Holt, Chief Justice of late Stuart England.

On the warm spring day of my visit, beneath the cold, carved gaze of a once mighty human judge, a sparrow lay, as if asleep, on the stone floor of the chancel. Trapped and exhausted, it had died before the altar.

LEFT – St. Andrew's Church, South Lopham.

23

Colne calamities and reconstructions

If ever a catalogue of the calamities visited upon the people, towns and villages of the lands around the River Colne was drawn up, it would be a long list of misfortune. Destruction natural and human inspired – fire and plague, tempest and earthquake, invasion and civil war, witchhunt and siege – all have been included in the experience of this corner of Essex.

With unforecasted violence, the gale of October 1987 swept across marshes, saltings and creeks to strike All Saints, Brightlingsea. Standing on a ridge above Alresford Creek the large church was, until that night, veiled by tall pines. But those towering trees could not withstand the mighty wind and down they came, smashing parapets and lychgate. Some years before, little more than a mile away across the creek, the early 14th century church of St. Peter was consumed by fire. But the nature of man and his Christian Faith is to rebuild and at Brightlingsea the roof has been repaired and stonework reconstructed and Alresford has a new church.

Brightlingsea's medieval church with its memorials to mercantile success and tragedy has suffered before – in 1814 its roof fell destroying the 15th century clerestory. Around the walls are memorial tiles inscribed with the names of parishioners who have perished at sea since 1872. Other memorials of metal and stone reflect the success of merchants of earlier times with brasses to members of the Beriffe family and a huge marble monument to Nicolas Magens, German merchant, lord of the manor and City financier, who was made British by Act of Parliament during the reign of George II. Beneath clouds from which cherubs peer forth, a ship's stern piled high with bales disappears behind an angel while another chubby cherub sits upon a cornucopia.

Wivenhoe's church, surrounded by narrow streets which lead down to the quay, has fine Tudor brasses within its restored fabric following the destructive earthquake of 1884. A reminder of much older destroying eruptions is the little town which took the name of an obscure Anglo-Saxon princess who sought religious seclusion above creek and marsh which also bear the name – St. Osyth. She established a nunnery at Chich, as the village was known in the 7th century, but piratical

LEFT – the ruined church at Alresford.

pagan Danes sailed up the Colne in search of loot and cut off her head. In Norman times an Augustinian priory was founded to administer her shrine and after its dissolution, the abbey and its impressive gatehouse of flint and stone came into the hands of the Darcy family.

In the century that Osyth formed her convent, St. Cedd founded a monastery within the walls of the Roman shore fort of Orthona five miles away across the mouth of the estuary. He and his fellows brought Christianity to an area where, in other times, the gods of the Celtic tribes, Romans and Vikings had been worshipped. Colchester is rich in monuments to past cultures and conflicts. There are defensive ditches built to protect Camulodunum, the war god's fortress; the Roman gate and walls raised after Boudicca's hordes had massacred men, women and children in a temple dedicated to an emperor; the biggest Norman castle keep in the land and relics of a monastic past battered by siege artillery.

The keep on the site of the Temple of Claudius is now a museum and among its treasures is a gravestone bearing the figure of Marcus Facilis, a Roman centurion who died in this outpost of ancient empire around the time that St. Paul was composing his epistles. The town was fortified by the English against the Danes and re-fortified by Norman conquerors whose commander founded an abbey. Colchester's ailing medieval cloth industry was infused with new prosperity in Elizabeth's reign by refugee Flemish weavers of the new bays and says and St. Osyth suffered an outbreak of witch mania which spread to other villages of Tendring Hundred. Another Norman foundation was St. Botolph's priory which, like the abbey gatehouse and several medieval churches, suffered in the exchanges of cannon fire during the Civil War siege.

The struggle lasted for more than 10 weeks during the summer of 1648 with Royalist forces holding the town against a Parliamentary army. The cavaliers were starved into surrender and two of their leaders, Sir Charles Lucas and Sir George Lisle, were shot in the castle precinct. A memorial to these *two most valiant captains in cold blood barbarously murdered* is in St Giles' church. Within two decades of Matthew Hopkins' Essex witchhunts and the siege came the plague; later came earthquake and storms. Time has swept away belief in Camulos, Mithras, Woden and witches, but not the faith of rebuilders.

Thornham Parva's invaded idyll

Down a country lane a little short of Yaxley, which means cuckoo clearing, where the Roman road begins its gentle descent towards the Waveney river-crossing and the old White Hart coaching inn at Scole (what relief that must have been to bone-jarred travellers before the railways) you will come upon one of Suffolk's best 'olde worlde' scenes.

A gravel-drive which is fringed thick with daffodils in Springtime, leads to the stout timber gate of Thornham Parva churchyard. Dotted around are old farm houses and thatched cottages, fields and woodland; here is a picturebook church set in picturebook countryside – as long as you don't look eastward because there, just beyond the churchyard boundary, a file of electricity pylons like sullen, droopy-armed monsters tethered one to another, comes marching across the landscape.

Turn your back on those steely, angular invaders. The little church of coursed flint walls dating back to Saxon times has a roof of reed thatch, and the stumpy tower, snug beneath its own tea-cosy cap of thatch, rises no higher than the roof ridge of the nave. Three Norman door arches, plain but enduring, and windows of Saxon, Norman and later ages pierce the walls. Duck through the narrow north door of the nave – there are no aisles here – and inside is an air of homely intimacy.

From wall to wall across the nave and chancel it is only half a dozen paces and the furniture is a mix from centuries past – an early 14th century iron-bound ark, a font with simple tracery decoration, an oak screen of a century later, a Stuart pulpit, Jacobean sanctuary wall panelling and a miniature, bow-fronted gallery of Georgian vintage. But within this plain and undramatic setting are artistic treasures which had been hidden for centuries. The nave walls carry pictures from the 13th century and some appear to tell the story of St. Edmund, the martyred East Anglian king. There is a large-wheeled cart, four monks bearing a coffin and two more holding a crowned, undecayed head over a skeletal body. Watching all the activity is a wolf such as that, which, according to tradition, guarded the saint's head between its paws until the searching burial party arrived to take it away for Christian interment. On another wall is a Nativity scene with angel, shepherd and sheep.

The most prized possession, however, is the famous Thornham Parva retable, an altarpiece of nine arch-framed panels with relief patterns of flowers and foliage. The sinuous figures dressed in long, flowing gowns are pictured against alternating gold and chequerboard backgrounds. In the centre is a Rood group Crucifixion scene of Christ between St. Mary the Virgin and St. John. They are flanked by St. Peter with his bunch of golden keys and a finger-pointing St. Paul who leans upon a sword. Also shown are St. Catherine with her wheel, a bare-legged and bearded St. John the Baptist, St. Margaret of Antioch with a writhing, knotted-tailed dragon at her feet, and St. Edmund displaying the arrow symbol of his martyrdom. At the ends are two black-clad saints, Dominic and Peter Martyr, the latter with an assassin's blade buried deep in his tonsured skull.

This remarkable piece of early 14th century religious art, probably executed for a Dominican house, had been preserved by a Roman Catholic family after the closure of the monasteries. When it came to light in 1927 it was given to the little church by Lord Henniker who lived nearby of Thornham Magna.

There the church has been restored with a chillingly heavy Victorian hand. There are numerous monuments and funeral hatchments in memory of members of the Henniker family, some telling of their martial service in the Guards, while another recounts the fate of their manorial predecessor, Cornishman Robert Killigrew, Page of Honour, Brigadier General and host to Charles II. Killigrew was killed in battle in Spain. Another tells of the infant Martha who died in 1838 –

The tender plant shed forth its beauteous form;
Look'd round upon this boisterous world; found its
Chilling blasts too rough: droop'd its head and died.

Back at Thornham Parva, a stone incised with arcs, triangles, and lines shares the churchyard weather with old yews, limes and aging memorials; its only words are 'Basil Spence architect'. Sir Basil designed Coventry's new cathedral following the destruction of that city's Gothic predecessor in wartime bombing. Mercifully, Thornham's painted saints have their backs to the east so they never see the sun rise through those arcs of power lines and pylons.

LEFT – St. Mary's Church, Thornham Parva.

Salle – 'ye me see in soche degre'

It is easy to find Salle church. No matter from which direction you approach its great tower can be spied rising above the surrounding farmland. Big, grand and proud enough to be a cathedral, this famed church, built in a century of murderous dynastic struggles and foreign wars, stands not within the protective huddle of old streets and homes as do the churches at nearby Cawston and Reepham, or at the gates of the Hall as at Heydon, but almost totally alone amid fields.

Why so big a church in such an unpopulous landscape of scattered houses and farms? Why build a church that could accommodate many hundreds for just a few score souls? Such questions only illustrate how cavernous is the gulf of our understanding of our late medieval predecessors. For the Boleyns, Briggs and members of the guilds who prospered in the East Anglian economic boom of the cloth trade, what else was there, once they had acquired the necessities of life and some of its luxuries, upon which to expend their surplus. So they built to the Glory of God and endowed chantries, hopefully, to ensure the eternal well-being of their souls.

Once through the big west door below two feathery censer-swinging angels and string of shields, one looks down the length of nave and chancel. In contrast to the restriction of the churchyard, inside it is a confrontation with space, height, soaring arcades and pacific, soothing calm – only the regular beat of the clock mechanism invades the stillness. All the colours of the stone and wood are gentle and appeasing; dull pinks, tan browns, the silver-grey of age in timber; no paths of suburban staircarpet but old, enduring matting which merges into invisibility.

In the tower, from whence emanates that slow heart-beat of time, is a ringers' gallery with protruding crane beam to raise the font canopy. Both porches have a room above; one, the Lady Chapel, has roof bosses which include wild men o' the woods peering out of encircling foliage and, just outside the heavy, beam-bolted door a squint points straight at Wood Dalling's church two miles across the fields. The transepts, built by wealthy patrons, are where the altars of guild chapels once stood; one has a window blocked by a memorial to Edward Hase whose *inviolable adherence to the rules of Honour and Probity* did not stretch to first seeking ecclesiastical sanction. The less ostentatious memorials to 15th century patrons reflect frailty not pomposity. The brass of Thomas Roose shows him with eight sons while his wife and four daughters display sterner countenances. John Brigg, who is *cowched undir clay* in the south aisle, is shown naked in his shroud, warning *As ye me see in soche degre so shall ye be anothir day.*

The wine-stemmed pulpit which has been turned into a three-decker; old pictures on the screen; carved oak chancel stalls with animals and monkish heads (below); ancient doors pockmarked by the shot of 18th century hedgehog and bird eliminations; and roof of angels and nightmarish faces are but some of the features of the Towne of Saule's church. Here the pushy Boleyns began their rapid rise from farm to earldom and a palatial home at Blickling. Salle has brasses of some of that family's humbler members and, if old tales be true, the body of Anne who became a Tudor queen. Many places make counterclaims, none could offer such glorious tranquillity.

LEFT – Salle Church amid the fields.

St. Wendreda's sky of angels

March, a little town astride the old Nene, is at the heart of the Cambridgeshire fens – a terrain where the roads either run straight for miles beside the waterways or zig-zag sharply across the flat fenland. It is a land where the all-enveloping sky-dome stretches wider and further (sometimes with a storm-laden and oppressive belligerency) than anywhere else in England. Here church towers and spires, landmarks for miles in the level landscape, soar like giant, vigilant sentinels. Is it any wonder that when the people of March put a new roof on their rebuilt church of unique dedication they filled it with huge angels? Guarded beneath a 'sky' populated by a wide-winged heavenly host (albeit in oaken effigy) they could cast from their minds the perils of life.

In 1086 only a dozen peasant families lived at March, sharing an island just above the level of the encircling swamps and meres with the Abbot of Ely's manor of Doddington. But long before then St. Wendreda had founded her hermitage in the wild isolation of Fenland where the people were sustained by fish, eels and pigmeat. When Wendreda, an obscure figure who may have been related to East Anglia's royal family, died she was revered locally as a saint. Her remains were removed to Ely and carried with Edmund Ironside's army against the Danes at Ashingdon. The victorious Cnut gave them to Canterbury until, in 1343, Wendreda was returned to March.

The church which bears her name (the Victorians built three others when the town expanded) is the result of new building to receive the patroness's body. It is a mix of honey coloured stone dressed with ashlar with a 15th century brick and flint clerestory to light the roof. The cloud of angels – there are more than 100 of them – looks poised for take off from the decorated beams. Standing beneath canopies in the wall posts are the effigies of Apostles, saints and martyrs. The oldest thing in the church is the font decorated by four simple fleurons, a Norman relic from the time those dozen families lived beside the Nene in 1086; and the newest is a memorial to a young Australian pilot who was killed when he guided his crashing Stirling bomber away from

LEFT – St. Wendreda's Church, March.

the town in 1944.

St. Mary's, Doddington, of which St. Wendreda's was a chapel, has a landmark spire too, as well as its own roof angels. Its churchyard is crowded with 18th century headstones of individual panache and appeal (St. Wendreda rises from lawned emptiness). Doddington, once one of the richest rectories in the land, now shares its medieval church with Benwick whose Victorian building lost its tower through subsidence and then the remnant when the pews sloped alarmingly. Some of Benwick's Victorian glass is in Doddington's windows. A Victorian schoolmaster, who died after falling off his bicycle, is remembered by a brass in a church where the music comes from a theatre organ. Unable to afford a replacement the rector put an appealing advertisement in The Times and someone obliged. Across Cornelius Vermuyden's Drain is Chatteris, another Fenland isle where St. Huna, a devotee monk of Etheldreda, found hermit seclusion. The medieval church was much rebuilt shortly before the First World War.

Upwell and Outwell are waterside villages stretching for three miles along the banks of the Nene which divides them between two counties. Both stone churches stand close to the waterflow within churchyards of enduring grey-white old headstones marked with medallions, chubby cherubs and cartouches. Among them at Upwell lies a veteran of Waterloo who 'died of a decline' – so *stranger step lightly: tis a soldier's grave* is the warning. The old square tower was given an octagonal top when the rest of the church was built before the Black Death. The uncommon interior is heavy with Victorian atmosphere, the nave crowded with seats and two galleries which allow close inspection of angels in the roof. The Victorians had to do much repair work – they also had to take down the old spire and replace the east window blown in by a gale. They recorded that during the years of renovation it was *to the credit of the respectable inhabitants of Upwell that they forsook not the assembling of themselves together on the sabbath*. Only a decade before 67 of their neighbours died of 'Asiatic Cholera' and their memorial brass asks, *Reader! why hast thou been spared, to what purpose hast thou been left until now?* There are also much older brasses, two to 15th century priests and another for Jane Bell who must have been a most pleasing wife for she gave her husband 11 children and *never delayde by deeds and good usage to geve him content.*

Shadow of time in Constable Country

Time passeth away like a shadow – every church and churchyard is a testament to the truth of that statement on the porch sundial at East Bergholt. This is 'Constable Country' where tourists come in thousands hoping that time has stood still since the miller's son painted his idyllic scenes of a Stour valley Arcady. But they will see no haywain with metal-rimmed wheels fording the river near Willie Lott's cottage, no Suffolk Punches dragging corn barges upriver to Flatford Mill, no shoeless lads mounted on the backs of leaping horses.

The landscape, light and sky are as Constable painted them – and still the church bells are in a timber cage because the parish never did *bylde the stepyll*. Among the headstones of the Georgian generations, James Turner, who had his share of worldly care, sleeps in the dust with Will Quilter awaiting the *riseing of the just*. Inside Edward Lambe's effigy still kneels above eccentric epitaph but now he surveys a fastidious and pervasive restoration of the church where John, the son of Golding and Anne Constable, was baptised in 1776.

Externally East Bergholt's large church of early Tudor date is markedly impressive with bright walls of flint and brick and battlemented aisles. But the little town's woollen manufactory was beginning its decline into a less affluent supplier of yarn when they ambitiously began work on the tower in 1525. Failure to complete it is linked with the fall of Ipswich butcher's son, Cardinal Thomas Wolsey, which was itself a sympton of the steady movement towards the English Reformation. As at Dedham across the river in Essex, they planned a processional passageway beneath their tower (at Walpole St. Peter in Norfolk it passes beneath the chancel).

Constable's paintings and sketches of wagons loaded with the fruits of the harvest and scythe-swinging haymakers reflect the years when the Stour valley farmers were enjoying an agricultural boomtime. His father's watermill at Flatford then ground corn where fullers had formerly worked on the products of weavers' looms. The flour was taken by barge to Mistley ready for shipment to London. Profits and food prices soared during the years of war with Napoleon but soon another of time's passing shadows would make the toilers of

LEFT – St. Mary's Church, East Bergholt.

Constable's golden cornfields into paupers.

The young painter, too, had his share of worldly cares. He fell deeply in love with Maria Bicknell, the rector's granddaughter, who was 12 years his junior. They had to wait seven years before they could marry by which time John was 40. Their marriage lasted only a dozen years until 1828 when Maria died *leaving seven infant children to lament her loss in common with their surviving parent.*

Many years before another widower recorded his loss with a brass tablet which is now affixed to the wall of East Bergholt church –

What ere thou art, here reader see
In this pale glass what thou shalt be
Despised wormes and putrid slime
Then dust, forgot & lost in time.
Birth, beuty, welth may gild thy east
But ye black grave shadowes thy west,
Ther earthly glorys short liv'd light
Sets in a long & unknown night.
Here till the sun of glory rise
My dearest darke and dusty lyes
But clothed with his morning raye
Her polisht dust shall shine for aye.
Reader, first pay to this bedewed ston
The tribute of thy tear & then be gon.

Even recognition of Constable's art by the Royal Academy was delayed and grudging, and in 1837 the painter went to his grave, not among the stiles, stumps and lanes he loved or near the sound of water escaping from mill dams, but near his wife at Hampstead. His stone bears no wordy eccentricities like Edward Lambe's who *all his dayes he lived a Batcheler well learned in Devyne and common lawes with his councell he helped many: yett tooke fees scarsse of any.* Flanking this epitaph are columns of words playing on the initials of this generous lawyer who died in 1617 – *Edward ever envied evill endured extremities even earnestly expecting externall ease; Lambe lived laudably Lord lett like life learne ledede livers lament.*

Time's passing shadows have been benign to Constable's country. In the world beyond, human expectations and life's pace have changed which is why the tourists come in search of his Arcadia – and for the days when the sun fails to cast a shadow on the sundial, there is a clock above the unfinished 'stepyll'.

The Tread of Harpley's Generations

How many foot-treads by generations of men and women, boys and girls, does it take to wear away an inch of stone doorstep? That was the unanswerable question which flashed to mind as I reached for the old handle of the wicket door with one foot in the smooth, concave curve created over centuries by untold thousands of soles stepping and standing, scraping and scuffing that stone.

Pass through the porch of flagstone floor and old, cold stone seats along its walls, place one foot upon the step where an inch of stone has been invisibly worn to dust by the tread of leather and reach for the iron handle of the wicket. For almost six centuries these thick, heavy timber doors – tracery-carved with canopied figures, lion and stag – have guarded Harpley's church which John de Gurnay, both rector and patron, enlarged in the good years before the Black Death.

After that pitiless plague had condemned countless thousands to untimely death another rector, John Drew, and a super-rich war-hero of the French campaigns, Sir Robert Knollys, rebuilt and extended Master Gurnay's work. The nave walls grew higher with clerestory windows, a new roof arose adorned with shield-bearing angels, the south aisle was refurbished and that porch was built with its wicket-embracing door.

The tower at the western end of the Knollys' aisle allowed the rebuilders to give the nave a large west window so that now, at the closing of the day, the light pours through old pictures of saints and clear glass onto the shiny black ledgers, many to generations of the Raven family, which patchwork the floor around the font. The church fabric retains features of John de Gurnay's 14th century work – in the south aisle a sedilia and piscina and in the chancel there is another sedilia with double piscina brutally hacked and mutilated with Reformation zeal. Also in the chancel is a priest's door through which John must have passed while Isabella of France, she who was dubbed the 'She-Wolf', plotted with her lover earl before being banished by her son, Edward III, to dream harmless dreams behind the draughty stone walls of nearby Castle Rising's keep.

The furniture of later ages stirs the imagination. Open the wicket and there stands a bulbous stove such as old soldiers watched glow red in darkened barracks and a funeral bier like a giant's pram, given by the people of Harpley to commemorate the 1935 Silver Jubilee of their royal neighbour, King George V, who loved Sandringham more than anywhere else on Earth.

On the panels of the old chancel screen are the repainted figures of Old Testament prophets – Amos, Ezekiel and Zachariah, Jeremiah, Jonah and Joel and others – fashionably attired as prosperous and worldly English entrepreneurs of the 15th century. The nave benches have been silent witness to many a change in fashion since the time carpenters made and then decorated them with traceried backs and mitred human figures, fanciful beasts, birds and a dragon (below).

John Martin sat at the front in 1638; his name is cut into the side of his bench, and nearly 150 years later Christopher Spurgeon began his long tenure as rector. In death he lies beneath the chancel floor; in life, we are told, he was a man of *'uniform and unaffected piety, benevolence of heart, suavity and kindness of manners'*. Another wall tablet tells of a tragedy at sea – the death of a later rector's son, only 16 years old, who fell to his death from a ship's rigging while a midshipman on a voyage to India.

LEFT – St. Lawrence's Church, Harpley.

The Ages of Man along the Lark

Thus doe I all the day, says the young hunter; *Thus doe I while I may*, say a pair of cuddling lovers; *Thus did I when I myght*, ruefully remarks an aging bystander; *Good Lord, will this world last ever?* groans a bent-backed, life-weary ancient. These sour and vinegary wall pictures of the Ages of Man were painted at West Stow Hall during the high summer of Elizabethan England.

In the 20th century relics far older than the West Stow frescoes have been uncovered in the valley of the Lark, the river which once gave Bury St. Edmunds access to the sea. Along the Lark's westward way from Suffolk's highest hills, past heath and breckland to the fens, are sites from the Stone, Bronze and Iron Ages as well as ones of Roman and Anglo-Saxon occupation. There are barrows, Roman potteries and villas, and the pagan Anglo-Saxon village at West Stow where thatch and timber houses such as those in which peasant farmers of the 5th and 6th centuries lived and worked have been constructed. There have been finds of coins, and, in 1942 the 'Mildenhall Treasure' was unearthed.

Of the three Fornhams, one, St. Genevieve, lost its church after a fire two centuries ago. It was near the church in 1173 that knights loyal to Henry II charged and scattered an army of mercenaries led by the rebel Earl of Leicester and his ally, Hugh Bigod. Culford's church, a Victorian rebuild, stands close to the school which was once the home of Lord Cornwallis whose surrender at Yorktown in 1781 ensured independence for the American colonies. In the church are notable memorials to members of his family. While Sir John Croftes, Master of the Horse to Mary Tudor, Queen of France and Duchess of Suffolk, was building West Stow Hall, another Tudor hall was being constructed at Hengrave by Sir Thomas Kytson, a rich London merchant. The Hall, now an ecumenical centre, stands close by the former village church which has a round Norman tower. The church was much rebuilt in the early 15th century and houses many large and impressive monuments to occupants of the Hall where John Wilbye of Diss entertained the household with his madrigals and music. The churches at Flempton, once served by a rector who must have rejoiced in his name of Blastus

Godley, and Lackford, where the Icknield Way crosses the Lark, were heavily restored in the Victorian period.

Across the heathland near Cavenham are the Black Ditches, linear earthworks near the Icknield Way as it approaches the river crossing. Icklingham has yielded many Roman finds – kilns, villa, coins, a lead baptismal tank marked with Christian insignia, and a small church of the time when Rome's rule in Britain was failing. The village has two churches – St. James which was thoroughly renovated in 1864, and All Saints, a thatched church of Norman origin but now redundant. Bright, its spaciousness emphasised by a stony emptiness, All Saints has changed little except for furniture since the 14th century when the aisle was built and the medieval tiles of the chancel floor were new.

In 1610, when John Speed drew his map of Suffolk and wrote, *The Aire is good, sweet and delectable: the Soile is rich, fruitful, and with all things well replenished, in a word nothing wanting for pleasure or profit*, he showed Lackford Hundred dominated by sand hills and empty west of 'Mildnall' and 'Lakenheathe'. It is still a largely empty fen landscape though now Mildenhall and Lakenheath have vast American air bases as neighbours. Before the Lark joins the Great Ouse near Ely it passes Worlington and Isleham; at the first a pillar of the church is carved with 'Crusader' graffiti and in the tower hangs one of Suffolk's oldest bells, made by Johannes Godynge of Lynn, before the Black Death. At Isleham, where many a white-robed baptismal candidate has been immersed in the river waters, the church has its old lych (corpse) gate, a roof full of wooden angels and memorials to benefactors, including the graceful brasses of the Peyton wives.

Mildenhall and Lakenheath churches are both noted for their angel roofs; at Mildenhall the heavenly figures survived a Puritan peppering of buckshot and an arrow or two. Mildenhall's church, which grew large during the medieval centuries, has the tomb of Sir Henry Barton, Lord Mayor of London, who, in 1405, ordered the capital's first street lighting of lanterns from All Saints' Day to Candlemas. At Lakenheath are 15th century benches carved with animals, older wall paintings including one of St. Edmund, and a large 13th century font. Unlike the cynical West Stow artist, the founder of one of Lakenheath's medieval bells gave it a Latin inscription of hope and faith – *Christ grant us ever a life of gladness*.

LEFT – interior of All Saints' Church, Icklingham.

'Devotion dwells not always in a cell'

If stones could speak what tales they might tell! Tales of conflict, compromise and harmony; riot and rebellion; peace and piety. The stones of Wymondham's abbey church have witnessed it all since the Norman baron, William d'Albini, established a priory near a tributary of the Yare in 1107. The d'Albinis had risen to the first rank of baronial privilege thanks to the favour of Norman kings and their own warrior prowess. The son of Wymondham's founder went on to earn the epithet 'Strong Hand' for deeds which became legendary, married a widowed Queen of England, gave an old castle as a priory of his own foundation and built new stone citadels at Castle Rising and New Buckenham.

Wind-bent churchyard pines and the shell of a tower hint at the sombrous arcades and triforium of William d'Albini's fortress of faith which he made a daughter house of St. Albans abbey where his brother was abbot. What stands at Wymondham now is but part of a once much larger complex of nave, chancel, transepts, aisles, towers, cloisters and chapter house. These old walls would tell, if they could, of human friction, often petty and bloody-minded, between parishioners and monks, vicar and prior, which at times enmeshed abbots, bishops, archbishop, and even kings and pope in unholy disputation. The root of the argument was that monks and townsfolk had to share the church.

In 1249 Pope Innocent IV gave judgement – nave, north aisle and one of the twin west towers were to be for parochial use, the rest was the monks' preserve. The monks built a dormitory over their aisle and pierced the wall with squints so that they could spy into the nave. After more than a century of 'peace' the dispute flared into life again when the monks hung their bells in the 'parish' tower, built a new crossing tower and masked the high altar and choir from secular view behind a wall six feet thick. When their new tower was ready the monks collected their bells from the usurped tower and then provocatively bricked up its entrance to stop the townfolk reclaiming their own.

Two could play that game! The irate parishioners broke into their own tower and installed their own bells which they tolled with vigour to give the monks sleepless nights. Then they blocked the doors between the bisected church to prevent the monks coming in to claim their share of the oblations. In 1409 the feud spiralled into riot until the law and the Archbishop of Canterbury intervened to calm the overheated tempers. Having agreed that there would be no further nocturnal bell-ringing, the townsmen raised a new tower for themselves (a few feet higher than the monks' tower) and built themselves an enlarged aisle and porch.

In 1448 Wymondham became an abbey independent of the abbots of St. Albans and harmony prevailed for 90 years until avaricious Henry VIII turned out the monks. Part of the Benedictine domain – central tower and south aisle – was incorporated into the parish church. The rest has disappeared except for the arch of the chapter house. The Black Monks' tower is now a ruinous haven for pigeons and their black-feathered brethren. The nave's 15th century hammerbeam roof is majestic with flowery bosses and rows of winged, wooden angels. A worn ledger to a young wife, Esther Le Neve who died in 1677, tells . . . *wisdoms not the child of yeares, so full of business & so pious well, devotion dwells not always in a cell*. More carved figures are in the north aisle roof including a grotesque pot-bellied female. Symbolising the restoration which ended the post-Dissolution decay is a huge, golden reredos (a memorial to the town's dead of the First World War) with Christ in Majesty surrounded by saints beneath a canopy of trumpet-blowing angels.

The end of the monks' tenure did not halt the violent days. John Flowerdew, the lawyer in charge of demolishing the monastery – a money-pocketing chance which he did not resist – was one of the landlords whose enclosure of commons sparked rebellion in 1549. A Wymondham townsman of some substance, Robert Kett, led the rebels who were bloodily put down in pitched battle. Kett (the name is on Wymondham churchyard headstones of later centuries) was hanged at Norwich and his brother suffered the same unjustified fate from Wymondham's highest tower. In the town are the Chapel of Saint Thomas Becket, a chantry of d'Albini foundation; the old Green Dragon inn and a Market Cross built in 1618 after a destructive fire.

Of those long-gone, quarrelsome, monkish days the kindest comment is to repeat the line of a memorial on the wall of the aisle once reserved for the parish – *Immitate his Virtues and forget his Faults.*

LEFT – the Abbey Church, Wymondham.

Ruined glory where the sea winds blow

Two churches, both dedicated to St. Andrew, the fisherman apostle, crouch low near the Suffolk coast within the investing ruins of their nobler predecessors. Gentle, salty, summer breezes and the cold, biting winds of winter pass unhindered through the glassless, empty window arches behind which the little churches seem to shelter. Where once there were coloured pictures of the saints, pigeons now perch for rest.

But the storms which caused these monuments of destruction came not only from the sea. Unlike Dunwich, where the North Sea's unrelenting tides have devoured churches, homes, and shops, the destroying tempests which brought ruin to the once large and resplendent churches at Walberswick and Covehithe were man-made and were motivated by fanaticism and greed.

The decline of Dunwich allowed both the rival ports to grab a bigger share of the lucrative sea-borne mercantile trade. Farmers and fishermen shipped their cargoes of cheeses and herrings to distant markets in the holds of barques which sailed to London, Iceland and out across the North Sea. And when people prospered in 15th century England so too did the parish church. At Covehithe, where the monks of Wangford Priory were the patrons, it was decided to retain the tower of their older, smaller church and build anew the rest with fine East Anglian chequer-board decoration around the walls.

At the more populous town of Walberswick a contract was signed in 1426 with master masons Richard Russel of Dunwich and Adam Powle of Blythburgh *to make a stepel* of similar design to the church tower at Tunstall with west door and windows modelled on those at Halesworth. During the several years of toil between each March and September (the feasts of the Annunciation and Michaelmas) the builders were given a lodging house, an annual payment of a barrel of herrings and 40 shillings of good English money, and all the necessary materials were supplied. By 1493, after yet more years of work by masons and carpenters, a new building had been grafted onto the 90 foot high landmark tower.

Walberswick had a church to rival in magnificence any of its rivals along the Suffolk coast. The town's other church near the river marshes and dating back to Saxon times was dismantled in 1473. But the prosperity did not endure. The coastal tides were relentlessly pushing up banks of shingle and clogging the river mouths with silt.

Covehithe lost is monastic guardians when Wangford Priory was closed and Walberswick suffered when the monks of Blythburgh were dispersed. The two big churches lost their tithes and although the Hopton family proved to be generous benefactors at Blythburgh and Walberswick, the years of prosperity were fading away. During the 17th century a new family of manorial landlords came to Walberswick with less than generous concern for the town and its people; they seized the common land, broke the heads of those who objected and set dogs on trespassers. With the men of Southwold, a new river channel was cut through the shingle bank but it failed to halt the decline. While King Charles I fought Parliament William Dowsing came to smash all things that he considered to be idolatrous in the church, destroying 200 picture windows at Covehithe and 40 more at Walberswick as well as ripping up brasses and leaving only their indents to be used as paving. Services were discontinued, the churches left to decay.

In both communities the battered churches were too huge and expensive for the dwindling number of parishioners to restore or maintain. At Covehithe the churchwardens, Enoch Girling and James Gilbert, put out the contract for a new but much smaller church in 1672. This church, the third to stand against the medieval tower, has nave and chancel of brick and flint beneath a thatched roof, all overshadowed by the ruined walls of older and grander aisles and chancel.

At Walberswick the story was similar – a diminishing population, many of whom were paupers, and a congregation of only 40 in a decaying church big enough for hundreds. Inevitably they petitioned that they be allowed to adapt the south aisle into a nave and chancel sufficient for their parish needs. So, a little more than two centuries after their forebears had celebrated the dedication of a fine and spacious building, Edward Collins and John Taylor, the *churchwardens in the eight years of the reign of our sovereign lord King William the third A.D.1696* presided over the conversion of the truncated aisle beneath a tall tower paid for in cades of North Sea herrings and lawful English shillings.

LEFT – church within a church, St. Andrew's, Covehithe.

'That Impossible Precept'

MAN KNOW THYSELF – 'that impossible precept' as Thomas Carlyle called it – is writ in golden capitals over the church clock at Methwold and anyone wishing to indulge in some meditative introspection could do much worse than practice it where the forests of Breckland edge towards the flat and anchoretic aloofness of the fens.

A calm, secluded and eminently picturesque spot is Cranwich where the little church and its circular churchyard occupies a slight rise near the River Wissey. Here the world-weary traveller can muse upon the words which once greeted supplicants to the temple of Apollo at Delphi in surroundings that would seem to many to be the epitome of 'olde England'. Was this round Anglo-Saxon tower a refuge for panic-stricken levies fleeing for their lives from battle with the Danes at Ringmere? On that day in May, 1010, Ulfcytel and his men faced the invaders but cowardly Thurcytel, known as Mare's Head, began the disaster by taking to flight leaving Athelstan, the king's son-in-law, Oswy, Wulfric and many other good thanes to fight and die with the steadfast men of Cambridgeshire.

The Norman nave, early 14th century chancel and later porch wherein swallows nest are all reed thatched. The interior is calm simplicity with plain medieval font and piscina, 17th century memorial slabs and an older altar stone with consecration crosses set in the floor near the initialled and dated stones of a 19th century rector's three daughters whose infant deaths are recorded on the chancel wall. The air of candid modesty is made complete by the harmonium with its two pumping pedals stamped as being 'mouse proof'.

A few miles westward at Methwold the Fenland influence is plain and the church tower, topped by octagon and spire, is a distinctive landmark within a lawned churchyard denuded of headstones. The porch with 1721 sundial leads into a mainly 15th century building. Inside are carved angels in the roof, an old iron-bound chest, and the incomplete brass of Sir Adam de Clifton which, so the story goes, was rescued by a parish hue and cry after a disreputable sexton had sold it to a tinker. The black and unflattering silhouette of lawyer Henry

LEFT – St. Mary's Church, Cranwich.

Partridge, who married two heiresses to Lynn merchants, is superimposed upon a marble memorial urn. Maybe his coffin was carried on the bier which tells it was *MAd By ME WIL AYARS* to the order of churchwarden *EdMUNd CANEY* in 1737.

Northwold, in contrast, has churchyard ranks of fine, individualistic headstones. The bequest boards tell of varied benefactions down the centuries for *proper objects of charity* – doles of bread; money to teach poor children to read the English Bible, knit and sew; to buy black or grey cloth to clothe paupers; a new church clock; repair of the causeway and the gift of Fox's Book of Martyrs and *a small Water-engine and five dozen of Buckets*. To revive the memory of Robert Burhill, who took sanctuary at Northwold *at ye breaking out of ye Troubles in October 1641*, a wooden plaque tells of his learned works writ in Latin and the help he gave Sir Walter Raleigh in writing a world history. Near a remarkable but battered Easter Sepulchre (of which Master Burhill would have disapproved in his blasts *against the greatest Champions of ye Romish Church*) is a memorial to a later rector of the village church. Richard Oram, who died in 1774, was a man of most respectable character *but whose sweet modesty of Disposition: while it added lustre to his merits, concealed them from himself*. Man, know thyself!

Ye weel disposyd men of Melford

Hard by a road along which Rome's cohorts marched is a broad village green which falls away towards the junction of brook and river. On one side are the rust-red brick walls of an Elizabethan hospital, on another more Tudor bricks create the turrets of a moated mansion. And rising over all are the battlements, patterned panels and window-filled walls of Long Melford's Holy Trinity. It is one of England's noblest sights – a huge, majestic ship of flint, stone and glass with its Lady Chapel prow aimed at every new sunrise.

The building is the proud product of business profit derived from the 15th century cloth trade. As at rivalling Lavenham, the super-rich merchants of this prosperous corner of Suffolk poured their excess into building and rebuilding their home-town church in glorious splendour. Cut into stone around the walls are inscriptions requesting prayers for the souls of the men and women *of whose goodis yis arche was made; dede these archis new repare; this chappell ys imbytylled.* The name which recurs is that of the church's greatest benefactor, John Clopton, whose descendants built Kentwell Hall.

It was with the money of the Cloptons, Martyns, parson Giles Dent, and *ye help of ye weel disposyd men* of Long Melford such as Richard Loveday, the Clopton's butler, that the church was rebuilt in the closing decades of the 15th century. The nave was extended, porches and chantry chapels added, and the years of building culminated in the construction of the Lady Chapel with interior cloister around a central shrine. The original tower was hit by lightning in 1710, rebuilt in brick and encased in stone and flint in the early 20th century.

The splendour of the church, however, is not confined to the achieved architectural ambition of the benefactors. Chief among Holy Trinity's other distinctions is the display of contemporary glass – saints, a lily crucifix, pieta, and kneeling donors, among whom are noble ladies such as the Alice in Wonderland figure of the Duchess of Norfolk in cloak and butterfly headdress, and men, some in brilliant heraldic dress, others in judges' robes. More portraits of the Cloptons are on the brasses and the effigy of Sir William, a staunch supporter of the House of Lancaster and veteran of Agincourt,

LEFT – Holy Trinity Church, Long Melford.

lies in armour. In the Clopton chantry chapel the tomb of benefactor John lies beneath statue niches, a frieze of shields and a canopy arch on the underside of which is painted a red-robed figure of Christ holding a cross-topped staff. Around the ceiling are linked scrolls bearing verses attributed to John Lydgate, a poet monk.

The most splendid monument is that of Sir William Cordell, wealthy lawyer, village benefactor and builder of Melford Hall where he entertained Queen Elizabeth during her cripplingly expensive royal progress through Suffolk in 1578. Cordell's mansion home later passed to the Hyde Parker family, many of whom held high naval rank and are commemorated by other memorials.

The large church built and beautified by the Cloptons, Martyns and others enjoyed only about 50 years of high splendour before the changes wrought by the Reformation in England ended the rich pageantry and ornamentation of the religion of their time. The niches where stood gilded statuettes of saints beneath carved stone canopies were emptied; wall pictures hidden under coats of puritanical wash; curtains and draperies of fine cloth removed, and the embroidered priestly vestments of damask and satin confiscated. Later, box pews enclosed by head-high panels from whose midst a three-decker pulpit erupted, filled the nave. Among the hatchments is an old survivor dated 1635. Beneath the coronet of Viscount Savage, after whose death it was hung in the church, it is charged with the many heraldic insignia of his family. Lady Savage suffered severely for her Royalist sympathies, having her home at St. Osyth Priory and Melford Hall ransacked by the mob.

The Lady Chapel, built in 1496, was a schoolroom for many years and on its wall is painted a multiplication table. Carved into the wall posts are figures of angels which must have heard children's voices recite the times tables in dinning unison. A relic of the rich iconographic furnishing so familiar to the clothiers of Long Melford is an alabaster panel relief. Now stripped of its paint and gilt, it shows the Magi offering their gifts of gold, frankincense and myrrh to the new-born Messiah held in the arms of his serene-faced mother. Peeping out from beneath the bedclothes are the faces of an ox and an ass. It had been concealed beneath the chancel floor and is now displayed upon a wall, in the words of Lady Chapel inscription, not to gain praise but that the spirit should be remembered.

Hospitallers' Church of rare shape

Her shape was rare: her beauty exquisit – so begins the inventory of virtues attributed to Lady Anne Deane by her son, Sir Dru. They are inscribed next to the white and spectral statue of the dame descended 'of ye Honorable Tribe of ye Druries' who died in 1633. The epithets can be applied to the land of gentle slopes, quiet villages and twisting lanes which separate the Stour and upper Colne.

Anne Deane's effigies, as well as those of her husband and children, are in Great Maplestead's old church but only a mile away is another church of rarer shape which is cool in summer but decidedly cold in winter. It was built by knights whose intention was (borrowing more of Lady Deane's excellent qualities) to be merciful of heart, helpful of hand, devout in prayer and pure in religion. They were the knights of the Order of St. John of Jerusalem or the Knights Hospitallers whose task was to protect pilgrims travelling to the Holy Land after the First Crusade at the end of the 11th century. The Order, whose members wore black cloaks emblazoned with a white cross, acquired estates in England among which was Little Maplestead where a Commandery of hospital, church, and domestic buildings arose.

The present church, built about 1335 to replace an earlier one, is on the model of Jerusalem's church of the Holy Sepulchre with apse, chancel and circular nave and aisles. It is one of only five round churches in England (another is Cambridge's Holy Sepulchre which is two centuries older). Now the picturesque and peacefully situated church, which was heavily restored in the 19th century, is all that remains of the Hospitallers' long tenure of the manor which ended with the surrender of the Order's properties to Henry VIII. The church was then made over to parochial use and the screen which hid the chancel, the knights' private chapel, from the nave and aisles was removed. The nave within a six-bay arcade is only 20 feet across and with surrounding aisles the rotunda the diameter is 30 feet. The surround and drip-stone of the west doorway has a decoration of three and four-petalled flowers. A rickety timber west porch, once used as a schoolroom, was replaced during the Victorian restoration when the old box pews and fittings

LEFT – the round church at Little Maplestead.

(but not the deep bowled Norman font for total immersion) were removed. The dormer ventilators piercing the roof over the aisles are a Victorian innovation.

Great Maplestead's church, dedicated to the hermit St. Giles, is also of unusual plan and much of it dates from the Norman period with Roman materials in the fabric. The apse and tower are Norman though the massy, stumpy tower has red brick repairs following a lightning strike in 1612. Chancel and nave were rebuilt in the medieval period when a south transept and aisle were added. Victorian restorers ended the decay and appended a porch, north aisle and transept but the dim interior lost its old fittings and gallery. Happily the brick-floored extension to the old transept which the Deanes built for their memorials escaped the heavy hand of 19th century up-dating. On one side lies the likeness of Sir John, his head supported by his right palm, and on a shelf above are the kneeling figures of his widow and six children. Gazing heavenward from the opposite wall is that eerie figure of his wife, Lady Anne, in her shroud beneath an arch of angels. At her feet lies the builder of this haunting monument, her son, Sir Dru (below), with wide lace collar overflowing his armour. Borrowing again from her long list of merits, he must have been a man of *judgment singular and devotions diurnal*.

Vailed wounds – What work was here!

Fifteen wide wounds this stone vails from thine eyes . . . so begins the bitter memorial to a 17th century murder victim in St. George's, Colegate. Norwich, the finest of England's major provincial cities, has suffered a thousand times fifteen 'wide wounds' – from Danish sack through plague, persecution, riot, rebellion, and religious bigotry to Luftwaffe bombs. The cathedral, castle, churches and narrow medieval streets which have witnessed every facet of the human condition are not 'stone vails' but eloquent assertions that no wound was mortal.

No English city wears its history so prominently as Norwich – a massy castle keep, lanes and plains, shops and pubs, city wall and Guildhall; and high over all the cathedral spire reaching 320 feet towards the heavens – 'its voice doth pierce the skyes'.

The town of wooden houses, 20 churches and some 5,000 people which had paid Saxon kings a tribute of honey, a bear and six baiting dogs, soon felt the thrust of Norman ambition. A hundred homes were cleared to make way for the castle near which a French quarter with market and church was established. In 1096 Bishop Herbert de Losinga began building his cathedral close to the Saxon market in Tombland and construction continued during four centuries. It is one of six English cathedrals to keep its monastic cloister following the dissolution when the Benedictine prior and convent were replaced by dean and chapter of prebendaries. Church and commerce were often in conflict and the citizens riotously invaded the monastery in 1272 and had to build the St. Ethelbert Gate as penance.

The city's prosperity attracted a Jewish community which settled near the castle whence they could retreat for royal protection during the sporadic outbreaks of mob fury. One such followed the alleged murder of a boy, 'St. William of Norwich', in 1144 (little St. Hugh of Lincoln and Robert of Bury St. Edmunds were similar local cults born of anti-Semitism). Medieval Norwich, guarded by nearly three miles of walls and 50 towers and gates which failed to keep out the plague (there were three major outbreaks in 20 years during the 14th century) or rebels, was a rich commercial centre, a home

LEFT – Norwich Cathedral, the west front.

to numerous monks and friars as well as a city of some 12,000 people served by almost 60 churches. The churches, some with parishes miniscule in area but dense in population, are a legacy of the city's vitality.

The 15th century heresy trials and grim processions of the condemned to fiery death in the Lollard's Hole beyond Bishop's Bridge were followed by the seizure of monastic estates, Reformation, Robert Kett's bloody rebellion and a revival of the cloth industry caused by the arrival of the 'Strangers' – refugees from Holland's religious wars. The city became a Puritan stronghold and the cathedral was a target of their censorious wrath. Bishop Hall recorded the destruction which occurred when they came in search of 'superstitious pictures and reliques of idolatry' – *Lord, what work was here, what clattering of glasses, what beating down of walls, what tearing up of monuments, what pulling down of seats, what wresting out of iron and brass from windows and graves!* Led by a lewd wretch in a cope, the vestments, organ pipes, surplices and service books were carried off to be burned.

For the Norfolk gentry, sections of 18th century Norwich were magnetic centres of elegant pastimes – theatricals, minuets and fashionable conversation; other areas were slummy, brutal and insanitary havens of disease. Banking, insurance and footwear flourished as the cloth trade decayed, overtaken by northern innovation and industrialisation. In art the skill of Crome and Cotman burned bright; in life the Christian compassion exemplified by Elizabeth Fry and, later, Edith Cavell, gave hope.

Norwich has so much to treasure from the past – noble St. Peter Mancroft and that host of lesser city churches, the Old Meeting House and Octagon Chapel in Colegate, Elm Hill and the Erpingham Gate are some. On a wall of the Great Hospital, which incorporates part of a medieval church, 'pious deeds' of Tudor monarchs 'to help decreped age in woful case' are gratefully recorded. Lewis Bryant, *barbarously murdered upon ye Heath near Theford* in 1698 lies 'vailed' beneath his black slab; arrogant Tudor propaganda obscures the truth. The hospital had been founded three centuries before by a bishop for 30 poor priests, lack-penny scholars and old paupers who were allowed to warm themselves by the fire. Bejewelled kings a 'generous bequest' (spoils of dissolution) could endow; the poor prayed for a glut of herrings.

Lynn and ye danger of ye seas

From salt marsh to rich, riverside port, Lynn's rise was rapid. *Rising was a seaport when Lynn was but a marsh* is a line of an old rhyme lamenting the hard times which befell Castle Rising as wooden-hulled merchantmen passed by to the staithes beside the Great Ouse.

Traders exported English corn, wool and cloth and their barques returned with Iceland fish, French wines, Baltic timber and Russian furs. A stone in St. Margaret's churchyard says of a young mariner who died in 1712 – *he hath gained his port and is at ease, and hath escapt ye danger of ye seas.* For the merchants of Bishop's Lynn, their minds no longer tossing on the ocean with their argosies of portly sail, ships safe in port beyond the danger of the sea meant profit; and the town has a noble heritage from those enriching days. In St. Margaret's church are two of the largest brasses in the land showing medieval mayors, Adam de Walsokne and Robert Braunche. They and their wives are accompanied by angel musicians and Adam's brass has scenes of rural life including a man bearing corn to a windmill, while Robert's shows guests enjoying the 'Peacock Feast'. St. Margaret's is a church of Norman foundation though much rebuilt, enlarged and repaired (as after the collapse of its spire in a storm in 1741). In the chancel are misericords carved with the faces of a king, queen, prince, bishop and wild man, while the levels of 20th century flood waters are recorded on a doorway. The 1754 Snetzler organ was installed when Fanny Burney's father was the organist; the Burneys lived close by but the oaths of the watermen sometimes forced Fanny to take her writing indoors.

Lynn quickly expanded beyond the limits of Bishop Losinga's grant on the edge of his Gaywood manor, and a new church, St. Nicholas' (a chapel-of-ease to St. Margaret's) was built near the Tuesday Market; its spire is a replacement for that brought down in the same storm which damaged St. Margaret's. Bishop's Lynn became King's Lynn when Henry VIII confiscated the property of the town's monks and friars. The town's medieval walls were repaired to meet the threat of the Spanish Armada but in 1643 they had to face English guns when the port was seized for the king by Sir Hamon le Strange of Hunstanton Hall. After a month of

LEFT – St. Margaret's Church, King's Lynn.

siege, blockade and cannonade the Royalists surrendered. Like Castle Rising, Georgian Lynn was a 'rotten borough' and the daughters of Lynn's rich merchants continued to be sought as wives sure to bring a worthy dowry (spendthrift Richard Gardiner, the 'Dick Merryfellow' writer of scurrilous pamphlets, tried but was rejected. His memorial is at Ingoldisthorpe).

Merchant's daughter, Margery Kempe, had been a different character – mystic and pilgrim, she wrote a book about her spiritual experiences. Pilgrims who came to Lynn on their Walsingham way called at the curiously shaped Red Mount Chapel, built in 1485. Not all Lynn's mariners were engaged in trade – George Vancouver sailed as a boy with Captain Cook and Fanny Burney's brother, and later he commanded an expedition mapping the coast of North America; while Sir William Hoste, as his memorial in St. Margaret's tells, fought with Nelson at the Nile, defeated an enemy squadron and forced the surrender of fortresses.

The Wash port which Lynn displaced, Castle Rising, is now more than three miles from the sea. Its Norman past is displayed in its church and the keep and bailey walls of William d'Albini's castle. Hard by the church is the hospital of the Most Holy and Undivided Trinity, a red brick Jacobean building ranged around a central court with its own tiny chapel.

Along the eastern edge of The Wash are churches of varying size, shape and age. Babingley's ruined church was replaced by one of thatch and corrugated iron by Edward, Prince of Wales, in 1894; Snettisham's medieval stone spire, a rarity in Norfolk, was above the crossing but the chancel has gone; and Heacham has a bust of Pocahontas, the Red Indian princess who married colonist John Rolfe. The little church at Holme-next-the-Sea is at the end of the Peddars Way and remembers Elizabethan Richard Stone and his wife whose 13 offspring gave them 72 grandchildren which they *to their greate comforte did behoulde.* At Dersingham, where the church has the tomb of a Tudor mayor of Lynn, John Chamberlane and his fellows spent two days of 1671 *in the flood gitting out of the cattell when the tyde did come over the top allonge the sea cost.* He asked that Psalm 29 (It is the Lord that commandeth the waters) be sung on the anniversary to put the inhabitants in mind of the mercies of God. John surely considered that Psalm singing, like that young sailor of Lynn, *never did no man no wronge.*

'Think on the glass that runs for thee'

Before steam power revolutionised travel and put the muscle of machines into industry, the transportation of materials in bulk was in the wooden hulls of ships and barges. Rivers were the arteries of trade so villages many miles from the sea could prosper if they had access to navigable water. North of Cambridge unnatural fingers of water – lodes – reach out to the Cam from villages on the edge of the fen to make them accessible to water-borne traffic. Reach Lode was dug by the Romans to give access to the Fenland rivers and for centuries the village at one end of the Devil's Ditch, the seven mile long Anglo-Saxon border defence, was the port for its neighbours. Later men dug new lodes to link Burwell and Swaffham Bulbeck with the waters of the Cam. These villages, whose names recall battles and invaders of the past, have relics of quieter times.

At Swaffham Prior two churches stand a few yards apart within the same churchyard on the ridge which rises above the village street. Such an unusual but not rare juxtaposition – Reepham and Willingale have pairs of intact churches, at Stowmarket, Middleton and Trimley in Suffolk and Antingham and Gillingham in Norfolk, one of the pair has vanished or is a ruin. The usual folkloric explanation of two pious but quarrelsome sisters fails when the building dates are compared. Swaffham Prior's churches, St. Mary and Ss. Cyriac and Julitta, have been restored and rescued from ruin. The two distinctive towers are an arresting sight, St. Mary's rising from a square Norman base via octagonal stage to a 16-sided top crowned by a modern spirelet in place of its lightning-hit predecessor; St. Cyriac's 15th century tower with imitative octagonal top was used as a bell tower when its nave was demolished at the 17th century union of the parishes. After the lightning strike in 1767 St. Mary's was allowed to decay and St. Cyriac's acquired a new nave but both buildings have been restored.

A glass screen divides St. Mary's old tower from nave of wood block floor, simple benches and windows which depict war machines and scenes of the First World War. Among the brasses is Robert Chambers, Gent, in high boots and Stuart costume, while memorials tell of refugee John Allix and his sons – one died an infant,

LEFT – the two churches at Swaffham Prior.

another after a fall, another *exhausted by a lingering illness*, and a fourth at the Siege of Badajoz *bravely vindicating the insulted rights of All Nations against the Tyranny & Oppression of the French*.

Swaffham Bulbeck (from the Norman Hugh of Bolbec who ousted the Saxon Alwy the Harper) had a nunnery but it was only a memory when a new lode brought river traffic to the mercantile offshoot at Commercial End. A more substantial relic of medieval monasticism is Anglesey Abbey (really an Augustinian priory founded in the 12th century) at Lode. Long before the men of Burwell dug their own lode, their village history had been closely linked with the Fenland abbey at Ramsey. A spring fed the defences of a fort (hence the name) near the spacious 15th century church which is renowned for its roof. Mounds mark King Stephen's 'castle' where Geoffrey de Mandeville, outlaw Earl of Essex, was fatally wounded in 1144. Mandeville had seized and fortified Ramsey abbey during his rebellion and, a chronicler monk tells that the walls oozed blood until the sacriligious occupation ended. A brass of Ramsey's last abbot rests in Burwell church where the roof carvings include curious elephants, illustrating the medieval carver's problem in depicting beasts he had never seen. Among the old churchyard memorials is a stone to 78 people who went to a village entertainment in 1727 and were burnt to death when the barn caught fire; one for a brokenhearted widow who *drain'd a cup of sorrow*; and others for boys and girls – *think on the glass that runs for thee . . . the moment when our lives begin we all begin to die*.

Bottisham church, dating from a century after Roger de Mandeville's death, has a macabre memorial to a brother and sister who died in 1638 – strangers in a world which *they tasted, liked it not and bad farewell*. A century later, when Sir Roger Jenyns died, tastes were different; he smiles and holds his wife's hand, both seemingly ready to retire to read their books in bed. Sir Roger (one of his descendants survived the Charge of the Light Brigade) ordered a charity sermon to be preached on the anniversary of his wife's death with relief for 20 poor folk who came to listen. He also founded a school and the figure of a Georgian schoolboy stands above the words *I was naked & ye clothed me*. A few miles away at Burrough Green an almost identical statue stands on the old school beneath the same words, but here he has a girl companion.

Kedington and the First Roundhead

An octagonal clock with one hand, a tower scored by the marks of an old, steep-pitched roof, a warm mix of stone, brick and flint in the walls, and a cobblestone porch floor arouse both curiosity and anticipation. Here on a ridge overlooking old mill house and a bridge across the Stour, only a few miles from where the river trickles out of 'high' Cambridgeshire to become the border between Suffolk and Essex, is Kedington's church of St. Peter and St. Paul.

The valley of the Stour is uncommonly blessed with churches of 'special' interest. Upstream is Little Bradley's dim and tiny Norman church with round tower (a curiosity in these parts) wherein lies printer John Daye – *the Daye that darkness could not blind*; downstream are Cavendish and Clare; Long Melford, Sudbury, Bures and Nayland; Stratford St. Mary and Dedham. To be notable in such company is to be notable indeed.

It is inside that the many delights of Kitten (as the village used to be called) are to be discovered. In this church, built on a site where Romans once raised brick walls, the generations of the past thousand years and more have left the marks of their times. Here is a Saxon cross sculpted when the martyrdom of Edmund of East Anglia was still alive in the memory of the men and women who had been his subjects; Norman stonework; medieval woodwork; Tudor roof; Jacobean pulpit; Georgian gallery and much, much more.

Brick floors and a medley of benches and box pews greet the incomer. A bow-fronted gallery for the village musicians is at the western end of the nave above rising tiers of benches where Victorian children once sat and shuffled under the silencing glares of schoolmaster and schoolma'am who had their own appointed places. A three-decker pulpit with hat pegs, wig pole and hour glass stand faces the canopied and compartmentalised comfort of the Barnardiston pew. Its front is from a 15th century screen and in its tracery are birds and dragons, foliage and faces.

A long line of Barnardistons presided over Kitten's fate and their memorials and hatchments have caused this place to be called Suffolk's 'Westminster Abbey'. Two, each a Sir Thomas, lie in armoured effigy next to their wives on tomb chests, and another of that name lies near kneeling wives, piled skulls with bones gripped in their teeth and pieces of his armour. Beneath all the end of a coffin seems to be vanishing into the wall. First to see the sun rise is the grim-faced *Image of Lyfe* of young Grissell Barnardiston with startling coiffure (below). She died in 1609 and her epitaph tells that she was *too wise in choice too olde in youthful breath; too deare to frendes: too much of men desier'd therefor bereaft us by untymely death: while shee trod Earth shee rais'd her mynd farre Higher, Her actions faire, unstayn'd of vice, or pride.*

Among other Barnardistons remembered here are Sir Samuel whose youthful, cropped head, it is said, inspired the quip, "What a handsome young roundhead is there!" from Queen Henrietta Maria so originating the term applied to Parliament's supporters to the Civil War. His father, the Puritan Sir Nathaniel, the religious and patriotic 'ornament of his Countrey', is shown holding his wife's hand and another memorial tells of a Sir Thomas who travelled *to Jerusalem and the most remarkable places of Syria and Palestine and the Seven Churches of ye Lesser Asia* before returning to home to marry and have six sons and six daughters.

LEFT – Church of St. Peter and St. Paul, Kedington.

Nat Willsher of Thaxted commends . . .

By whichever road you approach Thaxted, dominating the skyline in front of you is the soaring church steeple to guide you to the heart of the old town. The javelin point of the spire, its edges notched by three tiers of dormer windows, rises from its battlemented tower and flying buttresses to 181 feet above the churchyard – the church is less than a pace longer than the steeple is high. For those with time to linger, Thaxted and nearby villages of the upper Chelmer have much to admire from centuries when the tempo of life was seldom faster than the plodding pace of a horse and cart.

Thaxted's medieval richness resulted from the town's cutlery industry making swords and knives (the road which swings up the hill to Cutlers Green to the west gives a memorable view of town, church and windmill). Enhanced by cloth trade profits, of which nearby Saffron Walden was a major centre, and not least the patronage of the powerful Earls of Clare, whose title to the manor descended to the Crown through the Yorkist line, Thaxted acquired one of the most magnificent late medieval church buildings of eastern England.

The best approach to the church is up the cobbled lane from the 15th century Guildhall with its oversailing top storey and open groundfloor where traders set up their market stalls, transgressors were caged in the town lock-up and long, iron-hooked poles to pull off burning thatch were stored ready for the almost inevitable roof fire. Ahead lies the church of nave, aisles, transepts and chancel chapels built or renewed during the 14th and 15th centuries. South of the churchyard are two rows of almshouses pointing at the other dominant feature of Thaxted's skyline, the windmill, built during the wars with Napoleon. The two vaulted porches, one marked with the arms of Lionel, Duke of Clarence, the other with those of Edward IV, have rooms above and all who enter from the north must pass the caution Nathaniel Willsher left –

To thy Reflection Mortal Friend
The Advice of Moses I Commend
Be Wise and Meditate thy End.

Wide and bright, the interior dispels such gloomy (and hopefully premature) rumination. The spaciousness is

LEFT – Thaxted Church and the cobbled lane approach.

emphasised by the absence of old furniture and memorials – the nave has little other than a font and a canopied Stuart pulpit. There are stone seats in the transepts, and the Tudor portcullis is among the roof bosses – Henry VIII gave Thaxted to his first wife, Catherine of Aragon, as part of her dowry. Some old ledgers pave the floor, some with calendars of mortality. One lists six of John Rayner's 15 children with their ages, tabulated in columns headed years, months, weeks and days ranging from three years to three hours with one 'anonymous' daughter left blank. Another tells that in 1771 Daniel Haddon *had scarcely laid the adjoining stone over his Parents when he became the Subject for one Himself. Our life upon earth is as a Shadow*, it says; and Nat Willsher's caution is on the porch wall when you leave!

A little west of the Chelmer is Chickney's isolated and unspoiled little church with red-tiled Saxon nave, pyramid-capped tower, farmhouse floor and a wheel of candles hanging from a roof beam. A mile away upon a hill is Broxted's church with lancet windows in the old nave and memorial to Thomas Bush whose 'diligent attention to business' brought him a fortune, which he apportioned among his heirs with no less attentiveness. Tilty's church was the 'chapel before the gates' of the 12th century Cistercian abbey. The chancel, a huge window in its east wall, rises above the nave roof which has a cupola at its western end. Among the 16th century brasses are men in armour with their wives and children. Little Easton has a fine collection of monuments in its mainly 15th century church.

Within Little Dunmow church, once the Lady Chapel of an Augustinian priory, lies the dust of Robert Fitzwalter, commander of the barons' army against King John. It was Robert, so tradition asserts, who began the award of a bacon flitch to a man and wife who *in a twelve month and a day, repented not in thought any way, but continued true and in desire as when they joyned hands in holy quire*. The chair in which winning couples were paraded is in the church and a floor tablet recalls the infant, first-born son of a judge sent into the country in the vain hope of escaping the 'rageing pestilence' in London in 1665. With little more than leather buckets, thatch hooks, nosegays and pomanders to fight fire and plague, the twin terrors of generations of townsfolk, perhaps Nat Willsher's and Dan Haddon's words were not so pessimistic as realistic!

Glaven days that have been 'snacht away'

Around the arc of the East Anglian coast the churches of towns and villages close to the sea have their records of the authority of the waves over the lives of men. Some list the daring rescues performed by lifeboatmen, others, by their memorials to wealthy merchants, proclaim the affluent rewards of trade. There are associations with famous men of battle – notably Nelson at Burnham Thorpe – while Dunwich, Orford, Castle Rising and others are testaments to vanished greatness. The ruined churches at Covehithe and Walberswick are relics to the decay of community fortunes and there are countless personal memorials to individual tragedies, as at Winterton, where a parish priest died while rescuing a drowning choirboy.

The medieval churches of Cley-next-the-Sea, Wiveton and Blakeney, set within the same square mile close to where the River Glaven finds its way to the sea, illustrate all these aspects of oceanic demeanour with intriguing tales of the past when sails sought fair winds for profit not pleasure. A fire in 1612 destroyed a hundred homes near Cley church giving impetus to the community's shift to cottages closer to the sea as embankment, reclamation and silt shrank and ruined the haven below the old stone bridge. So now, between Cley and Wiveton churches, where ships carried off the products of harvest and loom, cattle graze beside a gently gliding river.

Cley's church is a product of different centuries – 13th century chancel, 14th century nave, aisles and clerestory, and early 15th century south porch which is superior to most in the county. It bears the shields of noble patrons and, on a roof boss, an illustration of one of life's hazards of centuries past – an old weaver-woman chasing off a chicken-stealing fox. Just inside the door is a foot-worn reminder of a shipwreck off Salthouse in 1720 when William Shepherd of Wisbech and most of his crew lost their lives in *A Sudden and Violent Storme*. The young man's memorial concludes, *I in my youth was Snatcht Away, Therefor Repent, make no delay*.

In the hillside churchyard, near the ruined and empty south transept, which is itself a memorial to the days when the port prospered, stands the tomb of Richard Greve who was rewarded with his own command and a

LEFT – St. Margaret's Church, Cley-next-the-Sea.

gold medal from Charles II for his part in burning the corsair ships of Tripoli in 1676. It should be remembered, however, that Greve's mariner predecessors at Cley had shown their own freebooting enterprise by seizing foreign ships. From the church's medieval past are the carved bench ends, chancel stall misericords with initials of the Greneway merchant family and the arcade figures of minstrels and St. George and dragon.

St. Mary, Wiveton, has a shrouded skeleton brass as well as its own link with the Greneway family. When he died in 1558, Raulf bequeathed weekly doles of 13d in cash and bread to the parish poor and around this benefactor's name arose the story of a foundling child who, like Dick Whittington, went to London in search of his fortune. Raulf certainly made money in London, not as a hopeful vagabond but a member of the Grocers' Company. Upstream, along the beautiful Glaven valley, Glandford's ruined church was rebuilt by Sir Alfred Jodrell whose shell collection is in the nearby museum. At Letheringsett is the death mask of the inventive blacksmith turned clock-maker, Johnson Jex.

Blakeney church has records of lifeboat rescues, a landmark west tower and a smaller beacon tower for seamen. Salthouse's church, much rebuilt in Tudor times, looks out across marshes reclaimed by blocking the Mayne Channel whereby the sea reached 'Saulthous port' as well as Cley and Blakeney. Here was born Sir Christopher Myngs who was killed fighting the Dutch in 1666. Samuel Pepys noted in his diary how, with tears in their eyes, a dozen lusty crewmen asked for a fireship to exact vengeance on their foes for the death of their commander. A few years after William Shepherd and his crew had perished when *forced on the shore in ye bay of Solthouse* and their bodies had been taken from the sands for decent burial, a memorial to Robert Colls and one of his three wives was put on the site of Salthouse's earlier church. They willed that on the anniversaries 10 shillings was to be given to the parson if he preached a sermon of *a full houre or the money not to be paid* followed by gifts of bread to the poor with one loaf for the clerke if he kept their memorial words clear of moss. They asked that *all should be fulfilled as long as ye world endure*. In the floods of 1953 it must have seemed that the world would not endure long as the sea 'snacht' away life and homes. Now, as for the survivors then, the church is a haven from the storm.

Fressingfield's defier of Kings

High Suffolk. A cornland where Romans built roads as straight as an arrow's flight and English lanes zig-zag to the navigational perplexity of strangers. Moated farm houses are broadcast across a townless land where some villages keep their old church at their heart while others are more distant, as though absconding from such company. Exploration here is rewarded by sights created long ago and the enduring marks of a family which rose from fish port traders almost to the throne of England.

At Fressingfield, where the churchyard dips away to a brook which feeds the Waveney, an old guild house shows its wall of red brick patterns to the stone and flint church porch built by an earl's widow whose husband had died of disease while fighting for Henry V in France in 1415. Six weeks later their eldest son was one of the few English nobles slain at Agincourt. Both the guild house, now the Fox and Goose, with the figure of St. Margaret of Antioch carved into a post, and the church endowed by the de la Poles were known to the village's most famous son, William Sancroft, Archbishop of Canterbury. Student, Fellow and Master of Emmanuel College, Cambridge, and encourager of Wren's rebuilding of St. Paul's Cathedral, Sancroft defied the king he had crowned, James II, and then, in loyalty to that deposed monarch, refused his oath of allegiance to William and Mary. *Deprived of all which he could not keep with a good conscience*, he retired to his Suffolk home where he died in 1693, and his tomb is near the porch beneath the text, *For as the Lightning cometh out of the East and shineth even unto the West, so shall also the coming of the Son of Man be.*

The great treasure of Fressingfield church is the array of 15th century benches with elaborate poppy heads and figures. Along the back of one are the crowing cock, scourge, nail, dice and other symbols of Christ's Passion. Another bears a chalice and the initials of Alice de la Pole, Chaucer's grand-daughter, whose husband, William, Duke of Suffolk, was brutally murdered as he sailed into exile. Of a later age, near the village pump and war memorial, is a fading sign which advertises loose boxes and horse and trap to let.

The long, wide nave of Laxfield church, standing hard by the old Royal Oak inn, guildhall and endowed village school, is full of Stuart woodwork and it was during the Commonwealth interregnum that puritanical William Dowsing, who was born here, went on his window-smashing, image-destroying tour of Suffolk's churches. There are box pews carved with dragons and long-nosed faces, Jacobean pulpit and reader's desk, and 'Seats for Young Men and Boys' which rise in tiers beside the Seven Sacrament font raised upon Maltese Cross steps. Dowsing's wife, Sybil, has a memorial beneath the chancel arch. Unlike William, John and Mary Borrett, whose lives ran concurrently with the Dowsings, bequeathed a *spotless memory* as well as a *fair estate and a numerous ofspring* according to their ledger. And – *as living they knew but one bed, so here they sleep in ye same grave after a sober, righteous and a Godly life of two and fourty years.*

At Horham, where the sweet produce of bees housed in churchyard hives supplements the church income, are old bench-ends and a Stuart pulpit. Wilby's pulpit is an elaborate piece of Jacobean workmanship and, on the older benches, are carved representations of the sacraments. In Worlingworth church, home of the village's 1760 fire engine, are a pulpit with suspended canopy and a superb set of 1630 pews. A picture shows the Georgian populace making merry at a village feast when a 50 stone ox was spit-roasted in jubilee celebration.

The de la Poles, whose fortune was advanced by marriage to Sir John Wingfield's heiress, built Wingfield's moated castle and the effigies of two of them are in the village church. Earl Michael, a victim of dysentery at Harfleur, is carved in wood beneath elaborate chapel arches cut with the de la Pole leopard heads and the Stafford knots of his wife's family. These emblems, with those of the Wingfields, are also on the font. Across the chancel, lit by its own clerestory and beneath squints aimed at the high altar and a helmet topped by the grinning face of a Saracen, is the alabaster likeness of John de la Pole in finely detailed armour. He lies beside his armless consort, Elizabeth Plantagenet, sister of Edward IV and Richard III. Their son, Edmund was Richard's heir and upon him were centred Yorkist hopes after defeat at Bosworth. But Edmund, a hot-tempered money-waster, was executed in 1513.

Unlike an infant remembered at Worlingworth, neither the high-born de la Poles nor Will Dowsing could claim they died with *No crime to answer, to expunge no stain.*

LEFT – Church of St. Peter and St. Paul, Fressingfield.

The Rose-Flower of Southwold

More than five centuries ago, when the partisan noble families of the Yorkist and Lancastrian factions were beginning to decimate each other in those eruptions of violence and treachery known as the Wars of the Roses, the people of Southwold did a deal with the monks of nearby Wangford Priory. In return for some land close to their new 'chapel', the Joyes, Bumbylls and all the other inhabitants of the hamlet agreed that every year in June, on the Feast Day of the Nativity of St. John the Baptist, they would bring to the high altar their annual offering of one Rose-Flower.

At that time, 1458, Southwold's new 'chapel' was nearing completion. Southwold was then not a parish but a dependancy of Reydon and its early 13th century chapel, built by Cluniac monks of Thetford Priory of which Wangford was a cell, had been destroyed by fire some 30 years earlier. Southwold's church of today is the joyous result of 15th century labours; certainly it is a joy to go back to again and again.

So much to see! Replica stocks by the gate remind of days when public derision was considered to be an essential element of punishment. Within a wide churchyard (thanks to that Rose-Flower land grant) rise tower and walls of stone and shining flint. Around the tower window arch the prayers of the patron saint are sought in letters individually crowned – SCT EDMUND ORA P NOBIS. Inside is bright space and colour – matt pale pinks and cream of stone, deep browns of polished woodwork, gold of slender-stemmed pulpit and roof angels.

So much to see! Hammerbeam roof with a host of angels, above the chancel it is boarded and painted with more angels bearing scrolls and symbols of the Passion; yet more of the angel host are depicted on the screen with further panels of the Apostles and Old Testament prophets. This treasure was sandbagged for safety during the Second World War when much of the Victorian window glass was destroyed by bombing. Now the story of St. Edmund's martyrdom is told in the glass of the great east window. Carved on the chancel stalls are contorted creatures, a rude face-puller and several heads of bearded old men in voluminous caps. Other wood-

work includes a 14th century chest with a mounted knight lancing a dragon, an Elizabethan communion table and, in the Lady Chapel, the roof boss faces of Charles Brandon, Duke of Suffolk, and his third wife, Mary Tudor, sister of Henry VIII, she with an antique bunched hairstyle. Mary, the beautiful English princess, had been married at 18 to a gout-ridden King of France who must have seemed very much an antique to her.

In Wars of the Roses armour, Southwold Jack stands sword in hand, ready to strike his bell, as he did long before they built the lighthouse, put the cannons on Gun Hill, English and Dutch fleets fought below the cliffs or the brief reign of the Brandon's tragic young granddaughter, Jane Grey. A brass tells of Christopher Younges, who died in 1626 – *a good man full of fayth was hee, here preacher of Gods word and manie by his ministrie weare added to the Lord*. His son John, who was of the Puritan persuasion, sailed away to found a Southwold in the New World of the Americas.

Oh! see how soon the flowers of Life decay.
How soon terrestrial pleasures fall away . . .

so says a memorial to an infant. At Southwold there is no decay but a church in full Rose-Flower bloom.

LEFT – St. Edmund's Church, Southwold.

'Choycest flowers fade with a blast'

Within just two square miles, beside the curving waters of the Great Ouse, are the four Wiggenhalls, each with its own church, although one is a riverside ruin and another is redundant. In two, where old memorials record past sorrows when 'the thred of life' was cut – *thus dread Heav'n its Empire will maintain, It may afflict; but Man must not complain* in the case of a Georgian schoolboy – the visitor can admire at close quarters the skill, imagination (and humour) of medieval carpenters.

There are stern-faced saints and martyrs; sinners being gobbled by the jaws of Hell; beasts and birds, and many jolly-looking fellows in flowing robes, some bearded, some in caps, one sitting cross-legged in conversation with his neighbour, another has head tight-wrapped and book in hand as though awaiting the dentist. These figures adorn the bench-ends at St. Germans and St. Mary the Virgin where the medieval seating is a match for any in the land. The larger figures of saints stand in niches created by 15th century woodworkers who chiselled into the flat faces of thick oak planks. The smaller figures were fashioned on the shoulders beneath swirling poppy heads, and the backs of the benches are richly decorated too, some pierced with patterns, others with ornate tracery.

The church with an uncommon dedication to St. Germanus, the fifth century bishop who quelled Britain's Pelagian heretics and won the bloodless 'Alleluia' victory over the Picts and Saxons, stands in the lee of the east bank of the river from which can be seen the ruins of St. Peter's. Among the 15th century bench-end figures at St. Germans are Apostles with their emblems – Andrew with saltire cross, Peter with keys, Simon holding a fish, Jude grasping a boat, John with a demon in his cup of poison – and Hell-bound vices shown as a lustful couple, a drunk topping-up his wine cup, and avarice with bags of cash.

There is also Victorian seating carved with episodes from the patron saint's life. From the 17th century are the pulpit and memorials to Thomas Moore the Rhymer and his daughters. Of Dorothy the father wrote *Summer fruits that ripen fast, very rarely long doe last, choycest flowers fade with a blast – she dyed as you and I must doe, sixteene*

LEFT – bench-ends at the Wiggenhalls.

hundred sixty two. Taking its inspiration from the breast-pecking pelicans which top old font covers (as across the river at redundant St. Mary the Virgin) is an epitaph to another of Thomas's daughters, Martha, who has two memorials – *Here's that Pelycan which did not spare to nurse her tender young with her heart bloud.*

A small heart-shaped brass marks the spot where, more than 500 years ago, a knight's heart was buried in the church of Wiggenhall St. Mary the Virgin. Sir Robert Kervile died abroad and his heart was brought back in a casket for interment in the family chapel. The Kerviles' Hall stood near the church which lies beyond the village with a Georgian Vicarage as its closest companion. Henry, the last of the Kervile line, has a large monument in the chapel; he died in 1624 and his armoured effigy lies next to that of his wife with their children below – infant son Gervase, with whom the line failed, is shown banded in his chrysom clothes and his older sister wears a scarlet robe.

Among the bench-ends decorated with lively and very human individuals, many of them in full-flowing Tudor attire, is one carved with the leopard heads and chevron of the Kerviles. The figures of saints include Leonard, the tonsured monk, patron of captives, holding book and shackles; Agatha, patroness of bell makers, with a knife at her breast, and Mary the Virgin and Mary Magdalene. Some of these saints recur on the rood screen.

The font cover, surmounted by a pelican in its piety, is dated 1625 and the brass eagle lectern is more than a century older, its inscription asking prayers for Brother Robert Barnard, a friar of Walsingham. Outside, where the cream-washed walls and fiery-bright new pantiles of the roof contrast with the weathered grey and brown stone of the old tower, churchwarden Joseph Rockley's sundial on the porch marks the passing of time as it has done since the days of Bonnie Prince Charlie.

At Wiggenhall St. Mary Magdalen, where long ago nuns of the Augustinian Rule had a riverside retreat, the church has its own collection of pictures of saints from the same century as its neighbours' benches but they are portrayed in window glass. Here was buried Francis Spensly who, in a long life 'above fourscore years' never suffered parental grief for *he knew neither the Cares nor the Comforts of a marriage*, ere, in Thomas the Rhymer's words, he became *part of heavens Eternitye.*

The stars of the Earls of Oxford

For six centuries the upper Colne valley was the Essex heartland of the de Veres' baronial power. Their citadel, the 100 foot high stone keep at Castle Hedingham, was built during Stephen's anarchic and lawless reign. They had smaller fortresses at Castle Camps and Great Canfield but while these strongholds of Norman conquerors are now grassy mounds or empty shell, the churches which the Earls of Oxford endowed still proclaim their patronage.

At Lavenham roof angels hold shields with the Oxford arms and more are on the porch, as is their boar emblem. Their heraldry can be found on fonts while their mullets or stars, such as those which gleam on the battlemented tower parapet at Earls Colne, are another signal of their influence. The earldom passed through 14 generations of the family, broken by occasional forfeiture, until the line failed at the death of the 20th earl in 1703.

Along the valley are churches raised by Normans and later medieval builders, some with Roman bricks in their walls and many with towers built anew or repaired with red bricks baked in Tudor times. Below that castle keep which stands gaunt but still strong within the remains of its moated bailey, narrow streets curve around Castle Hedingham's church. The huge brick tower, built in 1616, carries the shields of John, the 13th earl, who had a long and adventurous life. He commanded the right wing of the defeated Lancastrian army, which had two of the Pastons in its ranks, at the Battle of Barnet on Easter Day, 1471, when his men blundered through the fog and attacked their own side. Later he was locked up in a castle, escaped, and led Henry Tudor's army to victory at Bosworth in 1485 to end the Wars of the Roses. Restored to his estates, John de Vere enhanced Castle Hedingham's church and the star and boar are above the clerestory windows and in the woodwork of the hammerbeam roof.

The round doorway arches and uncommon wheel window in the chancel above three lancets indicate the late Norman origin of the building and this is emphasised by the aisle arcades and zig-zag decorated chancel arch which rises to a point. In the chancel are carved

LEFT – St. Nicholas' Church, Castle Hedingham.

misericords on the stalls and the black marble tomb of John, the 15th earl, whose likeness, with that of his wife, is incised in the top.

A mile away across the Colne is Sible Hedingham whose hillside church with de Vere mullet is approached up a rose-flanked path. Here is the hawk-decorated monument to a tanner's son who became the most famous mercenary of his time, Sir John Hawkwood. He learned his trade against the French at Crecy and Poitiers, went off to Italy where he hired out the lances of his White Company to the city state that paid the most and married a duke's daughter. Halstead's oldest church rises above the town's main street which climbs steeply from the river crossing. The church of St. Andrew dates from the 14th century when the town did well out of the wool trade but its medieval tower fell and was rebuilt.

Downstream from Halstead are four villages which take the river's name for themselves. At Earls Colne the early de Veres established a priory where they were buried when their spans were done. The effigies of three warrior earls (one who fought against his king under de Montfort's banner and two who swung swords in famous victories over the French) now lie in the shadowed silence of a little thatched chapel at Bures.

In a fold of the land through which an old millbrook runs down to the Colne is Pebmarsh whose 14th century church was given battlements and porch of Tudor brick. Inside is one of the earliest military brasses in the land – Sir William Fitzralph whose arms accompany those of de Vere and other powerful clans on the font at St. Mary's, Bures. The man who built Castle Hedingham's roof, Thomas Loveday, has his name on Gestingthorpe's hammerbeam roof. The church, which is of Norman origin, has a brick tower raised a decade or so after Earl John's decisive victory at Bosworth. Inside is a memorial to Captain Lawrence Oates whose self-sacrifice failed to save his companions on Scott's ill-fated 1912 expedition to the South Pole.

Below the stars and badges of the mighty de Vere earls atop the tower at Earls Colne is a tablet to a man *of humble station yet of sterling worth*. Servant and gamekeeper to the gentry for more than half a century, Abraham Plastow died in 1836 and some of his neighbours who *valued his unpretending worth* paid for his memorial.

Quaint, honest, simple-hearted, kind, sincere;
Such was the Man, to all our Village dear!

Benefactors and an unknown hero

Ye shall keep My sabbaths and reverence My sanctuary: I AM THE LORD – the words from Leviticus are writ bold above the door of Balsham's large church set in its wide, secluded churchyard. Here, where the land climbs from the Cambridgeshire fenlands towards Suffolk, in that triangle of high ground formed by rivers and the Icknield Way, there has been a church for a thousand years or more.

A chronicler long ago told how, after the Battle of Ringmere in 1010, one man retreated to the safety of the church tower to single-handedly fight off Vikings who had massacred all the other inhabitants of the village. That church where an unknown Englishman found sanctuary is no more but the bloody deeds of those times linked Balsham with the monastery at Ely, much to the benefit of the later medieval parish church. Among the English dead at Ringmere was Oswy, son-in-law of Brythnoth, the hero killed in the earlier battle with Danes at Maldon. Brythnoth was buried at Ely and his daughter, the Lady Leofled, who lost husband, son and father to Danish blades, added to the family endowments of Ely by giving the manor to the Benedictines.

Hugh de Balsham, Bishop of Ely and founder of Peterhouse, Cambridge's first college, in 1284, had a country retreat in his home village where he was host to Edward I. Under that king's grandson, Edward III, rector John de Sleford attained high office at Court (being in charge of the supplies of armaments) and the wealth which he amassed enabled him to greatly enlarge and enhance the church. The rood screen and loft date from his tenure, as do the choir stalls with carved arm rests of crouching animals and misericords faces (right), lions and dragon. Also in the chancel is this benefactor's superb brass with pictures of saints upon his cope, the arms of his royal patrons, and his soul being borne to heaven by angels. Close by is another large brass commemorating multi-lingual Welsh lawyer-priest John Blodwell who died in 1462. His cope, too, is decorated with figures of saints with more in the surrounding canopy; Asaph, David and Winifred emphasising the Welsh connection. An inscription telling of his law studies in Bologna and its practice in Rome, adds, with

LEFT – Holy Trinity Church, Balsham.

allusions to Old Testament texts, that earthly fame and fortune is vain and flesh withers like the grass.

Figures of John de Sleford and Hugh de Balsham are shown again in window glass and on the towering font cover carved by a 20th century rector, Canon Burrell. Also on the font cover are St. Etheldreda of Ely, St. Felix of Dunwich and Soham, St George of England with dragon, and Thomas Sutton, founder of Charterhouse.

Dr. Andrew Perne, the pliant Master of Peterhouse during the mid-16th century religious upheavals, left 10d a year for a Lent sermon and 40d to be given on Easter Sunday to poor children *who shall say their catechism best*. In the early 19th century destitute farm labourers rioted in Balsham and there were outbreaks of stack-burning and the smashing of machinery. On the church walls are reminders of those grim days if you were poor – the benefaction boards detailing Christmastide gifts of coal and clothing to widows and orphans. Some years ago a cross-inscribed Saxon gravestone was found in the churchyard – one would like to think that it covered the bones of Henry of Huntingdon's unknown hero who found sanctuary in the church tower when the plundering Danes came riding over the hill.

The wonder spared by 'Smasher' Dowsing

A salient of sandy heathland bounded by sea and rivers, its hem of marsh and shingle laced with creeks rich in smuggler tales – this is the land between the Deben and the Alde, along whose seaward side the tides have dragged the long finger of Orford Ness. Fourteen centuries ago Uffa's pagan warriors sailed from Sweden to the banks of the Deben to make Rendlesham the capital of their East Anglian kingdom and Sutton Hoo their cemetery. Uffa's descendants embraced Christianity, encouraged St. Felix in his mission and by the mid 7th century reign of King Anna, the father of several daughter saints, the Christain Faith was firmly rooted in eastern England.

At Ufford (Uffa's ford) a lane past cottage homes and cottage gardens leads to a churchyard gate beside the village stocks and whipping post. Inside the tree-shaded church is one of the great artistic treasures inspired by the late medieval Church in England. Soaring up towards the roof is a wooden font cover 18 feet high.

William Dowsing spared it twice. On his second visit he was kept waiting for two hours because the churchwardens William Brown and Roger Small, constable James Tokelove and sexton William Gardener would not give him the key. When he did get into the church, Dowsing found that the wardens had not carried out his destructive commands so he supervised the smashing of the windows, the pulling down of roof images and appointed new wardens. The cover, which he described as 'like a Pope's tripple crown', was saved. Some of the old glass has been restored to the windows and also in the church, which evolved from a small Norman building, is other exemplary woodwork which did not totally escape Dowsing's mutilation – hammer-beam roof with replacement angels, decoratively carved bench-ends including St. Catherine with her wheel.

There are more female saints including the little known martyr Florentia, on the panels of the rood screen. Sir Henry Wood's monument has the faces of garlanded bulls and three club-carrying wild men. The brass epitaph of Elizabethan goldsmith, Richard Ballett, is a cautionary piece fashioned before spelling was regulated –

LEFT – St. Mary's Church, Ufford.

Thow mortal mann that wouldest attaine
The happie havene of hevenly rest
Prepare they selfe of Graces all
Fayth and Repentance is the best,
Like thee I was somtime
But now am turnd to dust
As thow at lenght O Earth and slime
Returne to Asshes must.

The novelist rector of Wortham, Richard Cobbold, set the tragic end to his tale of Margaret Catchpole at Sudbourne and on other nearby beaches are Martello towers built to oppose a feared invasion by Napoleon's armies. Later at Bawdsey, where carelessness with fireworks set the church ablaze in 1842, experiments were conducted with a device to detect aerial intruders and radar was the result.

Orford has a castle keep and its church has the village stocks, civilian brasses and a ruined Norman chancel. The gatehouse of Butley Priory carries the shields of nations and baronial families, and Hollesley church displays in its oak pews the ability of modern carpenters to emulate medieval style. Boyton's church has the marks of Norman builders and stands by almshouses ranged around an open court. Overlooking the Deben is Ramsholt's rustic church of thatch and box pews. Its Norman tower, from which the sexton watched for the approach of the parson's boat, is round although your eyes may make you believe otherwise.

Woodbridge, for centuries a place of ship-builders and seafarers, is one of Suffolk's most attractive towns. It has a treadmill, windmill and a Dutch gabled Shire Hall given by Thomas Seckford, an Elizabethan benefactor whose tomb is in St. Mary's church. The 15th century building has a tower and porch rich in flint decoration and a big monument to Geoffrey Pitman who kneels Mikado-faced above wives and sons. Woodbridge men, sailed far to bring wealth and renown to their town and among them was John Fox, gunner of The Three Half Moons bound for Seville in 1563 when it was attacked by Turkish galleys. For 14 years he was a galley slave until, wielding a rusty sword, he led an escape by more than 200 Christian prisoners. They seized a galley, ran a gauntlet of fortress guns and sailed to freedom. Fox was rewarded by the Pope, came home in 1579 and told his tale to Richard Hakluyt, rector of Wetheringsett and recorder of navigations, voyages and discoveries.

Silence, music and legacies of the looms

Chance, coincidence and the emerging sunshine conspired to deepen the contrast. Beneath the grey gloom of a shuttered sky, narrow lanes high in the cow parsley and buttercups of early summer led to the out-of-the-way crossroads where a church had been raised by affluent weavers in faith and thanksgiving for their uncommon good fortune.

This was St. Mary's, Tunstead, where the light of day floods through huge windows to form slow-moving patterns on the stone floors of wide and empty aisles. The lonely silence of this church where, long ago, skilled artisans of the Norfolk cloth trade, secure and prosperous with an abundance of coins in their purses, had chatted and discussed, prayed and processed, is almost tangible. Or was it just imagination and the sad stillness of a church awaiting redundancy?

On the porch door a ring handle erupts from flowing tendrils of age-pitted ironwork fashioned long ago in the century of the Black Death and Peasants' Revolt. The trauma of that horrifying pestilence has left its mark on Tunstead. For more than 20 years the church had been abuilding when the plague brought everything to a halt. Two more decades passed before the work was restarted and so the wide aisle windows are of the pre-plague Decorated style while the piers of the nave are of later Perpendicular design. Along the aisle walls stretch lines of stone benches – 'the weakest go to the Wall' was the saying before 1400 when nave seating was rare.

The rood screen with its panels of saints was raised in 1470 when Henry VI and Edward IV both claimed to be king in England. Below the bricked up west window (a result of village vandalism more than 200 years ago) is an enigma – a platform with steps up at one end and, at the other, a door which leads down to a narrow tunnel-like passage lit only by a barred opening. Its purpose is a mystery but the likeliest explanation is that treasured relics were displayed on the platform and then securely locked away in the 'safe' below.

Outside the opaque blanket of cloud was breaking up as members of the latest generation of sheep nosed with their usual animal indifference among the headstones. On to Worstead, the little town which gave its name to a

LEFT – St. Mary's Church, Tunstead.

fine cloth, and the other face of this day of contrast.

Here, too, sheep strolled and lolled in the churchyard, burgeoning sunshine brightened the patterns amid the flints, a greeting smile from the vicar and triumphant music in the air as the organist rehearsed 'Jesu Joy of Man's Desiring'. Here, among monuments to the past, was the vibrancy of life and hope.

St. Mary's, Worstead, stands at the very heart of its small community – cottages, shop and houses, some thatched, some pantiled, cluster around. The clerestory windows permit no umbral shadows in the nave like those of Tunstead where the builders had finished their work a year or two before the industrious weavers of Worstead began their own project of church reconstruction. Twenty years later, in 1399, the year Richard II was kidnapped, dethroned and murdered, the people of Worstead could celebrate the fact that their new church, like their cloth, was one of the glories of Norfolk.

The screens of Tudor times are Norfolk glories too. At Worstead the panel pictures of Apostles and saints include another kidnap victim, William of Norwich, and the mythical Portuguese virgin princess, Wilgefortis, who grew a beard when her pagan father ordered her to marry. Also known as St. Uncumber, it was believed by medieval folk that she had the power to rid an exasperated wife of an unloved and unwanted spouse in return for an offer of oats. In the tower is a ringers' gallery of 1501 with inscription ending in the names of the churchwardens and the nave is lined by high-sided, draught-stopping box pews from the 18th century.

But for Worstead, as elsewhere in East Anglia, the prosperity founded upon the cloth industry and the skill of its weavers could not last for ever. Norwich became the manufacturing centre and a slow, gradual decline overtook the little town. Eventually even the hand loom weavers of Norwich were forced out of business, eclipsed by the mechanised mills of northern England. So decay and neglect afflicted the weavers' church at Worstead until modern restoration came to the rescue.

Now the weavers are back at Worstead, looms line one of the aisles where members of St. Mary's Guild of Weavers, Spinners and Dyers occasionally display the old skills. When I go to Tunstead again I hope not to have to borrow that big old key which goes in upside down. I hope the door will be open and more than just sunlight has cause to shine through the windows.

Gipping – tainted Tyrell's gem

A Suffolk lane that goes nowhere leads to a tiny chapel where flint, stone and glass glisten in the sun and their reflections are mirrored in the waters of a pond. Over a doorway, which carries the family badge and two entwined hearts, the visitor is invited to *Pray for Sir Jamys Tirell – Dame Anne his wyf.* Full of gentle colours, this remote and beguiling gem of Perpendicular architecture, is also tinged with the horror of the most infamous double murder in England's history.

The name Jamys Tirell links the Chapel of St. Nicholas at Gipping with the unproven if not unsolved murder of Edward V and his young brother, Richard of York – the Princes in the Tower – in 1483. He is the man blamed by many for overseeing the deed which allowed Richard of Gloucester to become King Richard III. Sir James Tyrell, knight banneret, eldest of the five sons of the High Sheriff of Suffolk and Norfolk, was a man with Hawkwood mercenary blood in his veins who 'sore longed upward'. The private chapel, built for himself and his family close to his Hall above the Gipping, was completed during the 26 month reign of his royal patron with whom Tyrell shared defeat but not death at Bosworth Field.

A plank bridge leads into the chapelyard – just trees and grass; no headstones because the Tyrells were buried at Stowmarket. Below the red-tile roofs are walls and buttresses of grey and black of chopped flints and white dressed stone with the occasional russet splash of lichen (the rendered tower is a demeaning later addition). The exterior abounds with shields, emblems and monograms which include the Tyrell knot, the linked hearts of his wife's family, the Arundells, and shields displaying the Tyrell's marriage alliances.

Light blazes through the wide clear windows onto plain cream-coated pews and pulpit, the smooth silvering browns of older artisan benches, one marked with the benefactor's insignia, and the dull, pallid yellow of floor bricks. In and around the east window are deeper hues – sparkling reds and yellows of glass pictures as old as the chapel, and dunnish blacks and browns of the classical mural of pillars and cherubs. Externally the small annexe has what appears to be a blocked window

LEFT – The Tyrell Chapel at Gipping.

but inside it is revealed as a fireplace. Sir James Tyrell's chapel was completed at about the time the two Yorkist boys were murdered in the Tower of London. Almost two more decades passed before Sir James Tyrell – either an eager accomplice to royal murder or victim of slanderous Tudor propaganda enshrined in Shakespearean drama – met his fate at an appointment with the executioner after being condemned for treason. Bosworth Field had ended the Wars of the Roses but aggrieved Yorkists continued with their plots, Tyrell being involved with the White Rose pretender, Edmund de la Pole, Earl of Suffolk and lord of Wingfield castle.

The Tyrell name which is also linked to the bowshot death, whether by accident or design, of William Rufus, appears on several memorials to later generations of the family at Stowmarket. The town's oldest church is a large but much restored 14th century building with tower and porches of the days when cloth making was concentrated in the town. Milton, it is said, visited his tutor at the Vicarage and, as at Christ's College, Cambridge, planted a mulberry tree. In later times a young and poor George Crabbe imbibed basic Latin and Grammar before his poetry and a parsonage brought fame and security. Ann Tyrell, shown shrouded on a brass, died in 1638 when she was only eight and was given an epitaph in rhyme –

High Heaven thou hast her & didst take her hence
The Perfect Patterne of Obedience,
At those Few yeares, as onely lent to show,
What duty young ones to their Parents owe,
And (by her early Gravity, Appearing
Full ripe for God, by serving & by fearing)
To teach the Old, to Fixe on Him their Trust,
Before their Bodies shall returne to Dust.

At Mendlesham, where one brook departs towards the Gipping and another flows to join the Waveney, the parish constables were ordered to muster the village militia for a day of military maneouvres in 1627. The equipment they wore is stored in the village armoury above the church porch, some of it dating from the time of the Roses wars. Perhaps John Turner, the village carpenter who fashioned the font cover and pulpit, was among the band of trained soldiers who marched off to Mellis Green on that August Wednesday morning. The carved benches are older examples of the skill of Suffolk carpenters, and also of wood are the two biers – one for adults, one for children.

Wheel of fire and wheel of fortune

Picturebook cottages, fine old houses and intimate old market place cluster around the edges of the churchyard. Towering over the little Broadland town of Ludham, and all else on the low, flat peninsula bounded by rivers, broads and marsh, is a noble church dedicated to St. Catherine, a saint of shadowy origin whose symbol is the wheel and whose name and torture we perpetuate at every firework display in whirling showers of sparks.

Testimonials to the turns of the wheel of faith and fortune abound hereabout. St. Catherine's wheel motif is repeated in the 15th century roof spandrels and in the earlier chancel is a sedilia with grimacing faces which remind of Charles Laughton's Quasimodo. Set high and low between chancel and nave are two 'treasures' – the screen towards which John and Cycyly Salmon gave 'forten pounde' in 1493 and, filling the arch above the rood beam, a reversible painting which was discovered hidden away and forgotten in the staircase to the rood loft by members of an historical society in 1879.

On one side is a crude crucifixion scene and on the other the heraldic arms of Elizabeth I between a crowned lion and a red, arrow-tongued dragon. The people of Ludham probably put up the hastily-painted rood group when Queen Mary ordered the return to Roman Catholic practices. But when her half-sister gave the wheel of history another nudge it was switched around to show the new allegiance – *VIVAT REGINA ELIZABETA* it proclaims. Pictured on the screen panels are two English kings, Edward the Confessor and Henry VI, and among the saints are Edmund of East Anglia, Walstan with his scythe, and two early Christian martyrs displaying the instruments of their torture – Apollonia with a tooth in pincers and Laurence with gridiron.

On the font are miniature figures, lions, and a bearded wildman with club and shield whose mate has long flowing hair. In the south aisle a squint is tunnelled through the wall near a mysterious protruding hand and, from font to chancel, lie a line of ledger slabs like a black carpet broken by a trio of small brasses. One tells in rhyme of Richard Barker of West Bilney, his *corps interrd as duste* till Judgement Daye, and another, heart shaped, remembers his daughter Grace. One ledger recalls

LEFT – screen angels at Barton Turf Church.

surgeon Richard Cooke who died in 1753. His courage, unwearied diligence and long experience *rendere'd him eminently successful in his practice and equal to almost any thing he undertook* which must have been a great comfort to his patients.

Across the river, from the tower of Thurne's little church, a squint hole is aimed at the gaunt ruins of St. Benet's Abbey, a once proud and powerful home of monks on the banks of the Bure. The isolated monastic house, amid the wet-lands of Cowholm, was destroyed by the marauding Danes who martyred King Edmund in 869 and Christianity vanished from the site until black-clad Benedictines returned during the revival of English monasticism in the 10th century. Royal favour enabled this oldest of Norfolk monasteries to prosper until a downturn of its wheel of fortune brought decay, ruin and a haunting place in Broadland folktales. The remnant of the medieval gatehouse is given a curious outline by the tower of a deserted windmill – an unwitting but apt reminder that Ludham's patroness, St. Catherine, is also the guardian of millers.

Broadland has other churches renowned for their chancel screens; some, perhaps, painted by artistic monks from that vanished abbey. Ranworth is famed for its screen with intricate pictures of Apostles and saints as, too, is Barton Turf's lonely church for its glowing portraits of the heavenly hierarchy of angels as well as saints which include Edmund and Apollonia. Beneath brass candelabra and paraffin lamps, fuelled ready for use should the electricity fail, a plate of brass is a testimony to Thomas Amys and his wife who endowed a chapel with *such godes as God had the seid Thomas lent*. He died in 1445 and left the warning *sum tyme we were as ye nowe be & as we be after this shall ye*. Outside a stone tells of a Boxing Day tragedy two centuries ago when four brothers drowned on Barton Broad.

Potter Heigham's attractively rustic church of flint, brick, thatch and round Norman tower has a screen of saints, as does tiny Irstead's church close by the River Ant. Here nave and chancel merge without an arch and overhead, between the rafters, is the underside saltire pattern of the thatch. Homelier and humbler than its grander neighbours, Irstead's church also tells the world, if less pretentiously, *Non Me Pudet Evangelii Christi* (I am not ashamed of Christ's Gospel) – words writ in capitals in Ludham's chancel arch.

The Poor Nun of Sithinga's Tale

How quickly man's deeds of today and yesterday slip away into history! Today's state of the art modernity is tomorrow's curiosity; ideas and artefacts, fashions and conflicts, sometimes even beliefs, become fossilised by time.

Seething's little thatched church, so obviously treasured by its community, makes the point as well as any museum or cathedral. The Norman round tower is topped by a needle spire of lead which beckons across the fields where, down the centuries, men and women have sweated and shivered with the seasons. Perhaps its flint wall was rising when a poor nun's claim to a four-acre patch somewhere in those fields was disputed by Isaac and recorded by the scribes of Domesday Book. She said – and the leading men of Loddon Hundred backed her claim – that the plot of land had been hers for years, held from Earl Ralph even before that foolish baron hatched rebellion at his wedding feast. The revolt resulted in a long siege of Norwich castle, the forfeiture of the earl's English estates and foreign exile. When the nun's claim was noted in 1086, the farmers of Sithinga had a conquering Norman king and a Bigod sheriff as their manorial overlords instead of an English archbishop.

Entry from the thatched south porch is greeted by a huge 14th century St. Christopher. Other wall paintings depict the macabre tale of the Three Living and Three Dead, Saint John the Baptist and episodes from the life of Christ. The seven sacrament font, its panels still remarkably distinct and lively, (mass illustrated right) and the surviving lower section of the chancel screen are of a century later. In the chancel are ledger slabs in memory of members of the 18th century gentry. That of Edward Osborne Esquire, adorned with dragon-topped arms, provocatively asks, *READER, would'st thou know more?*

The Georgian gentry – a class they themselves defined as 'between the nobility and the vulgar' – were seldom reticent in self-praise of their virtues or lineage, so we are told more, like it or not – *The Poor and the Distress'd Can testify his Humanity & Charity: He felt their Wants, And, He reliev'd them.* His niece's husband gained a less effusive and briefer epitaph – *He was a good Landlord, a kind Master; and Charitable to the poor.* From a pauper nun of an England ruled by conquering Normans, via the distress'd vulgarian subjects of Hanoverian kings even unto today, poverty, it seems, always escapes history's encapsulating powers.

Young men of more egalitarian temper are commemorated near the churchyard gate and by their flag of stars and stripes which hangs upon the nave wall. They came to Seething during the Second World War to make the air drone with the engines of slab-sided Liberator bombers. Beyond the village the squat, square, airfield tower which ordered their heavily-laden climb into the Norfolk skies is another reminder of the 350 American lives and the 146 then modern machines which mankind has had to enter in the wasteful debit column of war.

Brass paraffin lamps once illuminated Seething's Evensongs when the light of windows of different ages faded into winter darkness. Now those antique products of Johnson, Burton and Theobald are mounted on stands and adapted for electric light bulbs. Perhaps the brighter illumination they endow has a nuclear-powered generator as its creator.

LEFT – St. Margaret and St. Remigius Church, Seething.

'Silly Suffolk' and St. Edmund's Abbey

'Silly Suffolk' – that epithet which for those born beyond its borders conjures up images of slow-witted, monosyllabic, agricultural bumpkins inhabiting a time-locked landscape of haystacks, plodding horses and cottages masked by hollyhocks. But for Suffolk the word was justly applied and proudly worn. Our silly comes from sely, an Anglo-Saxon adjective meaning holy; to see a stone marked 'this sylly grave' is to confront the word without taint of implied mental incapacity.

For centuries the 'silliest' place in holy Suffolk (by repute if not always in practice) was Bury St. Edmunds, a town designed and ruled by monks. *The sunne hath not seene a citie more finely seated, so delicately upon the easie ascent of an Hil, nor a more Stately Abbey, in whose prospect appeareth rather a City than a Monastery, so many Gates for entrance, and some of them brasse, so many Towers, and a most glorious Church*, was how Leyland described the town. The saint's remains lay near the high altar beneath a huge model of a church covered by gold and silver.

The monastery was founded in the 7th century by the East Anglian king, Sigebert, who preferred the life of a monk. As Edmund's shrine it was enriched by kings and became one of Europe's greatest abbeys, the abbot enjoying almost princely powers as the master of estates larger than some counties. The produce of manors, tolls, dues and town rents, supplemented by profit from the pilgrim trade, enabled the abbots to build on princely scale. Land which had been under the plough when Saxon kings reigned was, by early Norman times, a growing town with a grid pattern of streets. On 40 acres bounded by walls and river a huge complex of monastic buildings arose around the great abbey church which was one of biggest medieval buildings in the land. As well as chapter house, refectory and cloister there were bakeries, breweries, treasury, mint and vineyard.

The 12th century gate-tower is the major survivor of the abbey's Norman structure. Of the abbey church, whose monks had relics and rituals to bring rain, prevent weeds growing in the cornfields, and remedy childlessness and headaches, little remains to describe its magnificence.

Grass grows where, on St. Edmund's feast day, 1214, rebel barons swore an oath to take up arms against King John. The huge church was destroyed piecemeal after the closure of the monastery because it was not needed for parochial use – the monks, having no desire to share their church with troublesome townspeople who, on occasion, violently invaded their precincts, had provided them with two large parish churches.

The Abbey Gate is a reminder of the factious relations between town and abbey. In 1327 a mob attacked the abbey and had to build the massive gatehouse as punishment; during the Peasants' Revolt later in the century the abbey was invaded again and the prior slain. After dissolution in 1539 the townsfolk continued to use St. Mary's, a church of mainly 15th century date, and St. James', which needed no tower as it used the Norman Gate as its campanile. Between the two churches is a tree-lined close with a modern statue of St. Edmund and memorial to later religious martyrs, the remains of the abbey charnel house with sad inscriptions and a wide, wild churchyard. St. Mary's has the grave of a Queen of France, Mary Tudor, who spent her final years at Westhorpe and whose body had been interred in the abbey which her brother closed. Almost 350 years after her death, Queen Victoria gave the church window glass depicting scenes from Mary's life.

From the roof wooden angels, saints and prophets look down on the memorials to knights and benefactors. There is a shrouded, wasted corpse sculpted in stone to the memory of John Baret who approved its design before he died in 1467. The beholder of this cadaverous creation is warned that he *may se hys owyn merowr and lerne for to die*. Also, beneath the decorated aisle roof given by John Baret and inscribed *Grace me governe*, is the brass of Jankyn Smyth who endowed a memorial sermon which has been preached every Thursday after Plough Monday since his death in 1481. St. Mary's also has a tablet telling that Peter Gedge, printer of the town's first newspaper, was *like a worn out type returned to the Founder in hopes of being recast in a better and more perfect mould*.

St. James' became a diocesan cathedral in 1914 and has been much enlarged with 20th century craftsmanship supplementing that of earlier ages, including the shields of earls and barons who, at the shrine of a king, pledged to fight their own monarch until he signed Magna Carta.

LEFT – Bury Bible

Three Acres of monks and soldiers

Nor love thy life, nor hate, but what thou livst
Live well; how long or short permit to Heaven.

Visitors lured to Castle Acre by the remains of a Norman stronghold and monastery tread close to these words when they enter the village church. They are on an old spinster's memorial set into the floor; and a more pleasing, pastoral situation for monks or men-at-arms to have lived well and left the rest to Heaven is nigh impossible to imagine.

Here, where Romans legionaries forded the Nar on their march along the Peddars Way, William de Warenne, Earl of Surrey, built one of England's strongest early castles as the headquarters of the vast Norfolk estates which were part of his reward for loyalty to William the Conqueror. The township, too, was defended by a rampart with parish church and churchyard just beyond its western edge. The Cluniac priory, founded by the second earl late in the 11th century, originally lay within the castle enclosure but the monks soon decamped to the peaceful meadows by the river. Of their church the west front, with its Norman arches and blank arcades, is an impressive remnant. In later years they added cloisters, infirmary, chapter house and other buildings and, in the early 16th century, the prior built himself a new house. But Heaven did not allow a long tenure and, in 1537, when only 10 monks inhabited the huge complex, the priory was closed and fell to ruin like the castle whose life had ended two centuries before.

In contrast to its silent contemporaries, Castle Acre's church of St. James has no hint of ruin or decay. It is mainly the result of the 15th century rebuilding of an earlier church with a screen, pulpit and soaring font cover of that period. The pulpit panels have pictures of the learned theologian saints Ambrose, Augustine, Gregory and Jerome while on the screen are the Apostles with St. Andrew's face peppered by buckshot; and peering into the chancel from a small, single-barred window is a skull.

If you be blessed with time to dawdle, walk the lane to the little bridge by the watersplash and head for South Acre's delightful church where a macabre charnel house of skulls awaits. Little has changed since 1725 when the Revd. Mr. Wm. Brocklebank *new pavid this chancel with stone at his own charge had the Gravestones Clean'd and laid even, Removid none that had any Inscription, but gave 3 plain ones to be laid in the body of the Church.* Three old stone coffin lids are still in the brick and pamment floor; half a dozen well-used old benches are in the nave below old paraffin lamps; the font is solidly Norman, and the Edwardian chancel stalls, carved with frogs, snails and otter, are the work of a more recent rector. The stone effigy of a cross-legged Knight Templar may be the Crusader knight, Eudo Harsyck.

A grandiose, colourful monument remembers Sir Edward Barkham, who obviously lived long and well, being Lord Mayor of London and buyer of the manor farm from the Harsycks in 1621. He lies next to his wife with the figures of his sons (below) and daughters separated by a pile of bones and skulls and above them all is a shrouded skeleton and hour glasses. Nearby are small slabs to a brother and sisters whom Heaven permitted but a few weeks.

A couple of miles downstream at West Acre are the remains of another Norman priory. Close by the gatehouse is the village church; its clockface has no numerals to mark the passage of the time which Heaven allows, instead the hands revolve past the letters *WATCHANDPRAY.*

LEFT – The ruins of Castle Acre Priory.

Royalists and 'lady old abbey by the sea'

HERE IS A STONE TO SITT VPON – these considerate words, weather-worn by more than three centuries of Suffolk wind and rain, are carved deep into stone in capital letters. When you go to Theberton, as you surely must, go on a day when silent airships of silver-white cumulus clouds drift across the sky; walk down the path between high, grassy banks topped by headstones, pass the churchyard lamp with its ironwork robin redbreast (you will discover its sad significance inside) and then, should you so wish, accept the invitation made long ago by honest John Fenn.

Royalist rector John was laid near the porch in 1678 *in hopes to rise to ye day of blisse and happiness*. The words go on to tell what happened to John when Cromwell ruled in kingless England – *turned out of this liveing and seqvestred for his loyalty to the late king Charles the First*. It was the fate of many of John's fellow clerics in those passion-filled and high-tempered days. Theberton church is still much as John Fenn knew it. Long, unbroken thatch from chancel to nave halted by round Norman tower with eight-faced bell stage pierced by four windows to let the chimes ring out and four blank ones for matching decoration. The battlements atop the tower and the flint-grey porch and aisle were built after another troubled priest of Theberton, John Doonwych, had departed after angry words with the Abbot of Leiston in front of his congregation in 1445. Inside is a Norman doorway, a font surrounded by hairy wild men and lions, medieval sedilia and aumbry and garishly painted arcade and chapel roof, but don't blame pre-Reformation painters, they had more sense and subtlety.

The memorials remind of later conflicts in faraway places of which the two rectors John had surely never heard tell. One remembers Col. Doughty-Wylie, soldier, saviour of Christians, war victim and Victoria Cross winner at Gallipoli. Certainly those priests of long ago knew nothing of the great continent of Australia where Col. William Light, a veteran of the Napoleonic Wars who spent boyhood days here, founded Adelaide. A suburb of that Antipodean city is called Thebarton; a heart-warming if mis-spelt tribute. In June 1917 the Suffolk night sky was fiery bright with the flames of a

LEFT – St. Peter's Church, Theberton.

blazing Zeppelin which crashed nearby after an encounter with a British fighter plane. The doomed German fliers were buried in Theberton churchyard for several years and in the church, preserved in a glass case, is a piece of their ill-fated airship.

A mile away is Middleton with houses protectively clustered around the churchyard which, long ago, was shared by two churches – the unsynchronised bell-ringing of two churches so close together caused disturbance to each other's services and complaint to the bishop. Fordley church has vanished; Middleton's remains, its font guarded by club-carrying wild men and the couplet *Cryst mote us spede And helpe alle at nede*. Across the Minsmere river another principled Royalist is remembered at Darsham. He was Sir Thomas Bedingfeild, a judge appointed by that unwise king to whom honest John Fenn was so loyal. This knight believed it was plain murder when Charles Stuart lost his head in the January cold at Whitehall in 1649 so *he layd down his place, and all public employment, retiring himself to this towne* where he died in the year the monarchy was restored.

Soldier, judge, cleric or commoner – death awaits them all. Samson Newstead's headstone says it with enviable honesty and bluntness –

A lump of dust alone remains of me
It is all I am. So all the proud shall be.

Along the Suffolk coast there are other reminders of the destructive powers of man and nature. At Leiston are the remains of the second abbey of the White Canons. The Premonstatensians had occupied a site at Minsmere in 1182 but the encroaching sea forced them to seek a safer home. In 1363 they rebuilt their monastery at Leiston, the only one of their Order in Suffolk, until dissolution ended their occupancy. But the original foundation, 'Lady Old Abbey by the Sea', had not been abandoned totally and one of the last of Leiston's abbots used it as his lonely anchorite cell.

The tides which threatened the Minsmere monks caused devastation at Dunwich. Once a major port protected by ramparts, most of Dunwich has vanished beneath the sea. Gone are its many medieval churches – the last, All Saints, was taken by the sea in the early 20th century. The houses of Knights Templars and Dominican friars have vanished and there are only scant remains of the second Franciscan Friary. Dunwich's latest church, built well inland, was consecrated in 1832.

Suspicion, resignation and true ensigns

Here boast nor Reader of thy Might
Alive at Noon and dead at Night.

The weather-worn headstone to a young wife and her babe carries these words below the decaying outline of a pedlar-knifegrinder in the churchyard at Helmingham. Not a quarter of a mile away is the Hall, the moated Tudor home of the Tollemaches whose grandiloquent memorials, safely protected from the erosive power of the elements, dominate the church interior. Their effigies – kneeling Elizabethans, a reclining 18th century 'Roman', a Georgian countess seated beside an urn and attended by tearful, pastoral child and lamb, the bust of a stiff-collared Victorian – reflect the monumental tastes of their times. The inscriptions tell of the triumphs and tragedies of a family which professed *an uninterrupted Male Succession from the Time of the Saxons*.

The church is mainly 15th century with a tower modelled on those of nearby Framsden and Brandeston. Breaking the nave roof is a dormer window into which pokes the top of the huge monument to four generations of Tollemaches, all Lionels, three of them kneeling in black Elizabethan armour and the fourth in his lawyer gown. Above each arch and window and upon the walls between are texts in blue, black and red letters which are the relics of dispute between rector and patron in the 19th century. In contrast to the Elysian monument to Maria, Countess of Dysart, is the martial memorial of stacked flags and cannons to son and heir Lionel, who was the only British officer killed at the siege of Valenciennes in 1793. Tragedy was heaped upon the House of Tollemache then because his father was slain in a duel, an uncle fell to his death from the mast-head of a man o' war and another went down with his frigate.

Also a victim of the wars with France was General Thomas Tollemache, fatally wounded in an attack on Brest 99 years before, *not without Suspicion of being made a Sacrifice in this desperate Attempt through the Envy of some of His Pretended Friends*. Close by in the shadows of the sombre Victorian restoration is the reposing life-size likeness of his brother, Lionel, clothed in Roman gown.

From Helmingham one of the Deben's tributary streams follows the gentle valley to Framsden where it passes an old windmill, thatched inn and village church before swinging away from the lane that leads into Cretingham. There the village street leads down to a bridge over the Deben above which stands a church of rare and unspoiled interior. It has no aristocratic stone monuments which seize the eye's attention – the memorials are few and modest – but the sallow walls, pale brick floor and the time-chastened blacks and browns of old box pews, worn benches and Jacobean pulpit.

From Cretingham bridge a lane imitates the twists and curves of the river which has its source beyond Debenham, an attractive little town whose heart is a rising street flanked by old homes, inn, school and guildhall. The base of the sturdy, square church tower which is filled with boards recording the achievements of past bell-ringers, has 'long and short' quoins by that Saxon race from which the Tollemaches claimed unbroken male succession. Later generations built the 13th century chancel, heightened the tower, added the galilee, rebuilt the nave and added the aisles. The pulpit is another fine example of Jacobean woodwork – in the troubled days of the Civil War the Royalist vicar was pelted with stones as he preached.

In the chancel the figure of Sir Charles Framlingham, builder of Crows Hall, a Tudor mansion a little over a mile to the east, lies beside his wife. Their moated home was acquired by Sir Charles Gawdy who loyally espoused the Royalist cause to *ye uttermost hazard of his life and fortune*. A brass tablet taken from the vault tells of Sir Charles' midnight exit in November, 1650, – *who in his time was blessed in the happie choice of a most vertuous wife . . . about twelve at night he departed, I cannot say hee died, for by a voluntary chearfull and devout resignation of him selfe into the hands of the Almighty to the wonder and astonishment of the beholders though he prevented not the stroake yet assuredly he felt not the bitternes of Death*. The nave has a memorial to an officer killed aboard a man o' war at Trafalgar. The Rev. John Simson's monument has words in Latin, Greek and English. He was a contemporary of Earl Lionel and General Thomas Tollemache who were *descended of a family more antient than the Norman Conquest*. Mr Simson's epitaph runs –

We boast not here (kind reader) a descent
From Brittish, Saxon, or the Norman race; . . .
Of honourable arms we in the room
Display, true ensigns for a Christian tomb.

LEFT – St. Mary's Church, Helmingham.

Ely, where God's train will take you in

For centuries it was difficult to get to Ely. The best way was by boat along the Cam or Great Ouse – that was how the monks travelled in 695 when they went in search of a stone coffin for their foundress, St. Etheldreda, and it was how they eluded angry pursuit when they stole the body of her sister, St. Withburga, from Dereham in 974.

Travel was easier and faster after the summer of 1845 when the railway came but the Christmas Eve 11.15 from Norwich that year never got to Ely. Driver Tom Pickering liked to open the throttle and his train came off the rails, killing him and the fireman, Richard Hedger. The railway's steam locomotives, which were instituting a revolutionary change in travel, inspired the 24 lines of rhyme put on their memorial – The Spiritual Railway – (although they got the unfortunate fellows' names wrong).

God's Love the Fire, his Truth the Steam,
Which drives the Engine and the Train . . .
In First and Second, and Third Class,
Repentance, Faith and Holiness.

An island of green-sand rising above surrounding fen and mere, Ely was an isolated retreat. Etheldreda, a daughter of a king of East Anglia, established her monastery in 673 and a tangible link with those earliest days of Ely's Christian history is the broken memorial cross with Latin inscription to Etheldreda's steward, the monk Ovin. Almost two centuries later the pagan Danes razed Etheldreda's foundation as well as Peterborough and other fenland monasteries. St. Ethelwold, the bishop who strove to revive monasticism in eastern England, re-founded Ely in 970 and at the Norman Conquest it was one of the richest abbeys in the land.

Ely's inaccessibility made it a rebel lair. Hereward defied William the Conqueror until the monks, faced with the confiscation of their estates, submitted. They then struggled to regain those of their manors which had been seized by Norman barons – the Pope ordered their return under threat of excommunication. In 1083 the Norman Abbot Simeon began building the third abbey church (the present cathedral) and during the 12th century Ely became an outlaw retreat once more when Geoffrey de Mandeville, Earl of Essex, terrorised

LEFT – Fenland glory – Ely Cathedral.

the region; a relic of those troubled years is Cherry Hill, the remains of a motte and bailey castle near the cathedral. In 1322 work on the new Lady Chapel had just begun when the central tower collapsed which led to the raising of Ely's architectural wonder, the Octagon and Lantern Tower.

The Reformation brought more savage destruction upon the cathedral – Etheldreda's shrine was destroyed, abbey treasure removed and the sculptured figures of the Lady Chapel pitilessly mutilated by Puritans. The chapel was given over to parish use to replace the demolished Church of St. Cross. Decades of decay followed; Oliver Cromwell, who occupied the Steward's House near St. Mary's Church, closed the cathedral and in the 18th century Daniel Defoe noted that the building tottered 'with every gust of wind' and was quite amazed that it had not fallen down.

From Palace Green with its Russian cannon, a trophy of the Crimean War, the cathedral west front of turrets, tower and tiers of blank arcades is an imposing spectacle which would be even greater had not the north wing of the west transept collapsed in the 15th century. Little old glass remains after the destruction ordered by Bishop Goodrich at the Reformation but much fine medieval detail survives – a 12th century Christ in Majesty above the Prior's Door, the tombs of bishops, misericords, chantries and Ely's *pick-a-back imps in glee, making mock at you and me.* Other buildings from the monastic past remain, among them the Ely Porta, a gatehouse begun in the reign of Richard II; Prior Crauden's Chapel which survived Parliamentary demolition by becoming a house; the monks' granary barn and the Bishop's Palace.

Most travellers to Ely now come by road, guided by the dominating silhouette of the cathedral rising above a flat fenland landscape. From Soham, where St. Felix founded a minster church 40 years before Etheldreda established her monastery, and then Stuntney, the road leads into the diminutive city at the point where, long ago, the causeway led to a drawbridge over the river. In Victorian England it was the steam locomotives of the railway which made travel cheaper, faster, if not always safer –

Come then poor Sinners, now's the time
At any Station on the Line,
If you'll repent and turn from sin
The Train will stop and take you in.

Queens, Shelton Church and Shelton men

One league long, half a league wide, 60 oxen to pull the ploughs, a few acres of meadow, woodland for some pigs and a church for 200 or so souls. That was Shelton when scribes compiled Domesday Book, William the Conqueror's tax gazetteer. Norman landlords, English peasant farmers, their wives and children, pigs and oxen, all are dust now. So too is their church. But in later times a family which took the village name as their own climbed the ladder of wordly riches and built the church anew.

Shelton's church of Domesday times had been replaced long before Sir Ralph Shelton began his joyous work of warm red brick patterned with bluish diaper and wide windows. Little more than the flint tower was retained from an earlier rebuild to which new porch, nave and chancel, two full length aisles and a sacristy were added. It is inside, however, that Sir Ralph's work of the time when Henry VII was patiently and prudently rooting the Tudor regime makes the greatest impact.

Light cascades from the clerestory onto bright white walls, arcades and pastel brick floor. Above the pillars are empty niches and, higher still, angels toting shields, some with the builder's rebus of scallop shell and tun. Now these little angels bear no wall posts because the roof was carted away to top a tithe barn. Sir Ralph died ere his plan was done and the stubby beginnings of his tomb canopy (and porch vaulting) betray the failure of the son to honour his father's wishes. Son John Shelton married Anne Boleyn, the aunt of the queen of the same name, and they became embroiled in the cross currents of intrigues at Court.

For a time Mistress Shelton was the harsh and abusive keeper of Princess Mary, daughter of Henry VIII by his first wife. Another future queen, Elizabeth, daughter of Queen Anne Boleyn, was hidden in the old church tower by great-uncle John when danger threatened. In the glowing red, blue and yellow of medieval glass in the east window Ralph and John are shown in their tabards and armour as they kneel in prayer with their wives. Nearby is a monument to lawyer Sir Robert Houghton, who purchased the Shelton's moated manor house. In judge's cap and robes, the dwarf effigy of Justice

LEFT – St. Mary's Church, Shelton.

Houghton kneels with members of his family beneath a comic skull and crossbones. The Shelton family-village tie ended when Maurice, 'last male heir of the family', was buried in the chancel in 1749.

In contrast to Sir Ralph Shelton's spacious and lucid late Perpendicular church, many of its neighbour churches still have round towers of Saxon or Norman date. Hempnall is an exception. There the Domesday assessors found that Ralph Baynard's large and populous manor had a priest and two churches and two mills as well as plenty of plough oxen, pigs and sheep, and some cattle and horses. St. Margaret's church evolved from one of those two Saxon churches, its medieval tower bearing early 18th century weathervane and clock.

Only the ruined base remains of Hardwick's Norman tower, the top fell in 1770. Fritton church has a St. Christopher wall painting, another of St. George mounted on a white charger despatching a dragon, with yet more dragons on the screen donated by John Bacon whose happy-faced portrait with wife and numerous offspring is painted thereon. Woodton has memorials to the Suckling family, Nelson's ancestors on his mother's side, and the headstone of a *stout and bold* huntsman who died in 1759. Master Baldry travelled far afield to display his art and *Few of his calling could with him compare For Skill in Hunting Fox or Fallow Deer.*

Bedingham church stands high and companion-like across the fields from Woodton. It is surprisingly large, roomy and bright inside with the gentle, muted colours of old benches and brick floor. Box pews line the aisles; many fine 18th century black ledgers to members of the Stone family are set in the floor; the font is stepped and lion-guarded; the chancel has sedilia and piscinas. A tablet tells of a young man *whose blooming virtues were faded by the nipping blast of a Consumption of which he died at Bristol hot-wells.*

On the rear benches are a flat-faced Tudor couple, she in a hood such as Mistress Bacon wears at Fritton, to remind that congregations used to be segregated. The round tower of Morningthorpe church stood before the Normans came to the villages of Depwade Hundred. Its memorials tell of a young naval man accidentally shot by a fowling piece and of young Henrietta who was only six when her epitaph had to be composed:

*In perfect innocence Life's slender path she trod
And with her dying Lips exclaimed I do love God.*

Norman painters and Tudor knights

One of the historically important results of Victorian and modern restorations of East Anglia's old churches (as well as the occasional accident) has been the uncovering of the medieval wall paintings which decorated the interiors of parish churches before the Reformation.

St. Christopher holding the infant Christ was a popular image and usually it was the first to greet the visitor, being prominently placed opposite the main entrance. Among other favourite subjects were the Doom or Last Judgement above the chancel arch, scenes from the life of Christ, pictures of saints, the Seven Deadly Sins, the Seven Works of Mercy and the Three Living and Three Dead. Encircled consecration crosses dating from the time when the church building was dedicated are relatively commonplace.

The purpose of the paintings, as was that of the glass window pictures, was to inspire, teach and caution the largely illiterate populace. Most of the wall pictures which have been revealed by the removal of Tudor whitewash are from the 14th and 15th centuries when English church interiors were filled with highly colourful, even gaudy, decoration.

A collection of much older paintings and in a very different style are in an isolated Essex church of unexceptional exterior. The wall paintings at Copford, particularly those in the vaulted apse, reflect the continuing influence of Byzantium on the Church art of western Christendom in the 12th century. The Bishops of London held the manor of Copford and their Norman church of vaulted apse, chancel and nave with Roman and early medieval bricks in its fabric was built during King Stephen's reign.

The paintings, which date from the time of the church's construction, were found during repairs in 1690 but they were covered over once more. During the 19th century the extent of the paintings was revealed and restoration undertaken. Only some of the original nave paintings have survived; others which completed the arrangement were lost when the roof vaulting was removed during the enlargement of the church with a south chapel and aisle in the 13th century. Dominating the apse is a ceiling painting of Christ in Majesty (left) –

LEFT – Christ in Majesty, Copford Church.

a bearded, red-robed figure seated on a throne of gold in an encircling rainbow held by angels. Between the apse windows are the archangels Michael and Gabriel and below them is a series of portraits of the Apostles. The underside of the arch is decorated with twelve linked medallions enclosing the Zodiac signs. Prominent among the subjects pictured on the nave walls is the Miracle of the Raising of Jairus' daughter.

A church which is a total contrast to Copford's dim, Norman austerity stands only three miles away at Layer Marney. The embattled, light-filled church with a giant St. Christopher wall painting was rebuilt in red Tudor brick by Henry, first Lord Marney, close to the towering gatehouse with eight-storey turrets which was to have been only part of his new residence. But Henry, who was high in the favour of Henry VIII, died in 1523 and, when his son, John, died two years later the family which had held the manor for four centuries was extinguished and their plan for a new mansion left incomplete. Whereas Copford is devoid of interior monuments, Layer Marney has the dominating tombs and black marble effigies of the two Lords Marney and the alabaster figure of one of their ancestors. John, the last of the Marneys, is also shown on a brass with his wife, Bridget, at Little Horkesley.

Finchingfield and its silent Squire

Life glided smooth adown its easy way for Thomas Marriott until the August of 1766 when Finchingfield gave him a tomb. The Pant valley, a landscape of appealing villages, old inns and cottages, farms and windmills, is, as Thomas Marriott surely found, a most pleasing patch of Essex in which to let life glide along. But not for everyone, then, nor in the years before or since, has life been such a gentle, carefree journey.

The church at Finchingfield, where the sturdy mass of its tower tells of Norman origin, has been buffeted by the world. When, in the mid 14th century, they sought to widen the building with a north aisle (the south aisle had already been made) the Black Death intervened. The project was completed in later years but the change in styles of the pillar mouldings is an unintended memorial to the calamitous interruption. The spire, lost in a storm, has been replaced by a bell cupola and, amid the armour, heraldry and plumes of Sir John Berners' brass, is a tiny monkey, the pet whose warning cries saved them when the house caught fire.

The memorial which rouses the most curiosity is that to William Kempe and his wife. It was put up 24 years after Kempe's death by *their nephew and heire intaild* (their only child, Jane, had married *with a double portion of graces and fortune* but no title to Spains Hall). William died in 1628 when he was 73 and is described as pious, just, hospitable and *Master of him selfe soe much that what others scarce doe by force and penalties, Hee did by a Voluntary constancy, Hold his peace Seaven yeares.* His vow to utter not a word for seven years resulted from his regret at having unjustly accused his wife of infidelity. Extraordinary mishaps are said to have occurred; once he fell off his horse and lay silent until he was found.

On the font are the arms of the de Vere earls whose carpenter fashioned the ornate rood screens. From the churchyard a path leads to the 15th century Guildhall and onto Church Hill. Below are Green, duck pond formed by a tributary of the Pant, houses of varying size and age, and, beyond, a post mill.

It was William Kempe who appointed Puritan preacher, Stephen Marshall, to Finchingfield's vicarage in 1625. Marshall went on to take an active political role during the Civil War years. Earlier, he had been preacher at nearby Wethersfield where, in a later age, Patrick Bronte was curate before moving on to Haworth Parsonage with his novelist daughters. Wethersfield church, much of it built before the Black Death, stands by a Green and has a short spire on its squat, late Norman tower. A tablet recalls Joseph Clerke who outlived five sons. For one of those sons life was no easy glide. Charles Clerke sailed with James Cook on all three of the navigator's Pacific explorations and when Cook was slain he *succeeded to the command of His Britannic Majesty's ships, the Resolution and Discovery* but died of consumption six months later when only 38 years old. He was buried far from his Essex home beneath a tree in Kamchatka.

Great Bardfield church, where each parishioner is prayed for once a month, stands on a hill above a village of timber-framed cottages, windmill, watermill and old shops. The building is 14th century as is its notable and rare stone chancel screen (there is another at nearby Stebbing). *Imortal life all hail! Corruptible life farewell* says the memorial to William Bendlowes, a Tudor lawyer. Little Bardfield's church has a flint and pebble tower built a few years before the Norman Conquest and Saxon windows in the nave.

Isolated among trees near the Hall is Little Sampford church with its rustic, unrestored interior. The Pecks, 18th century occupants of the Hall, are remembered by large monuments – mother Bridget reclining in a Roman gown, daughter Gartrude was taken in *the flower of her age* by smallpox as was brother Philip while serving *his prince and countrey at the greatest hazard* with the army in Ireland. Father William *liv'd with the devoutest piety* which, with his other attributes, were *virtues truly rare in the age in which he liv'd.*

*Lo in this tumbe combyned are thes toe bereft of lyfe
Sur Edward Grene a famus knyghte and Margerye hys wife.*

They died during the upheavals of the Reformation and their son Rooke, constant to his Roman Catholic faith, was fined and locked up for not going to church. Eventually the family fortunes were ruined; so, perhaps, Rooke Grene would have agreed with Thomas Marriott, who after a careless youth, concluded in his old age –

*That God alone is good; and man is frail;
That Wealth, Wit, Wisdom are a vain pretence,
And nothing fix'd but Truth & Providence.*

To know our proper stations

As the tree fell to earth, it still must lie . . . – the first line of a doggerel verse carved on an old man's headstone at Thurning a few years before Victoria, the teenage daughter of a duke, became England's queen. Then, as always, Thurning was really not a place at all; not a single cheek-by-jowl cluster of cottages and lanes but a wide scattering of independent farmsteads.

Like the felled tree which still must lie, the church of St. Andrew enjoys an uncommon stillness in its tree-shadowed seclusion. But in 1825, a few years before the four-line verse was cut into Tom Flood's headstone, the little church he knew had echoed with the sounds of activity and change. Carts filled with woodwork from a Cambridge college chapel were ending their slow journey in the churchyard of this truncated little church.

The chancel, built long ago when those troublesome Bigods were the earls of Norfolk, was recorded as being *undecent and filthye with durte* in Elizabethan times and later it fell into ruin beyond repair. Its 13th century east window and priest's door were built into the nave's eastern end and the tower and north aisle are work of the 14th century. Inside, however, is where the true delight awaits, the result of those cartloads of college chapel furniture transported from Cambridge.

Like many other Norfolk parishes, Thurning had links with the University town – in Great Snoring's church there are many monuments to Fellows of its patron college, St. John's, while Gonville and Caius College owes its existence to Norfolk parson, Edmund Gonville, and Norwich-born John Kaye (he 'Latinised' his name), who achieved fame as physician to Tudor monarchs. When, in 1823, Corpus Christi College began a massive expansion plan which entailed the destruction of its Tudor chapel, the college had held the patronage of Thurning for more than a century and a rector, the Rev. H.W. Blake, was a don of the college. With Sir Jacob Astley of Melton Constable paying the bill, unwanted chapel fittings from a college which had been founded by religious guilds soon after the Black Death, were conveyed to Thurning.

And so the little church acquired its splendid Georgian hierarchical interior. The panelled sanctuary

LEFT – interior of St. Andrew's Church, Thurning.

has a three-sided communion rail, box pews fill the north aisle with others for servants backed against the tower and a three-decker pulpit overseeing the plain, unmarked benches of the commonality. Everyone knew their 'place' in those days or, as Dickens put it –

O let us love our occupations,
Bless the squire and his relations,
Live upon our daily rations,
And always know our proper stations.

Squire and his relations from the Hall had the largest of the boxes at Thurning, directly opposite the pulpit and reading desk. Next to them sat the family from the Rectory and the other boxes were allotted to the farm households of the parish – Manor Farm, Rookery Farm, Craymere Farm, Burnt House Farm and so on. At the back are the boxes designated for Hall and Rectory servants and a small one, just inside the door, for the Rectory coachman. Until well into the 20th century other men and boys of the parish occupied the block of benches beneath a row of hat pegs while their segregated womenfolk sat across the gangway which is paved with memorials to their social superiors.

These shining slabs commemorate 17th and 18th century members of the Elwin family. In later years a daughter of the house married William Wake who went to India as a merchant, became the Governor of Bombay but died aboard ship on the way home. James Gay, who was also prominent in the 1825 refurbishment of the interior, fared better. He returned to his homeland after holding high office in Ceylon, bought Thurning Hall from the Elwins and lived to be 90 years old.

Forget not, however, that the Georgian elegance of Thurning's polished three-decker pulpit and box pews also reflects an English society which was as gruelling, vicious and uncaring to the majority of its citizens as it was indolent, refined and comfortable for a few. Ignorance was rife, old women were still attacked as witches, inquests returned verdicts of 'death by the visitation of God' on paupers dead of starvation, women and children gleaned the fields after harvest, poachers fought gamekeepers, smugglers battled with revenue men, the bodies of murderers were left to rot on roadside gibbets, rick burners were hanged and petty theft was punished by transportation to the other side of the world. One labourer who was found to have a rabbit in his bag told the beak that life in jail would be 'luxury'.

Ancient art along the Stour

The narrow, sometimes switchback lanes linking the villages between the Stour and its Suffolk tributary, the Brett, criss-cross a hundred square miles permeated with reminders of England's medieval past.

Here are timber-framed homes and guildhalls; marvellous churches endowed by wool merchants; humbler ones where Norman arches attest their age; effigies of knights in stone, wood and brass which describe the changes in the noble fighting man's armour; and on walls and fonts the mark of the de Vere earls. Effigies of some of the martial Earls of Oxford now lie in the shadowed silence of a thatched chapel built by Normans where Edmund was crowned King of East Anglia in 855.

At Wissington, close by the Stour in the flat valley farmlands, a small Norman church stands close by old farm buildings and a Georgian Hall built for a banker. With rendered walls, roof of red tiles and weatherboard bell turret, the old building was restored with 'Norman' fittings in the mid 19th century. The red, blue and golden yellow of the Victorian glass in the windows of the apse, which was rebuilt on Norman foundations, glow in the heavy-shadowed interior. The door and chancel arches are fine examples of Norman work. In their zeal to 'Normanise' the church, the Victorian restorers repeated the roundhead arch motif in the stone pulpit and woodwork of the nave stalls, choir benches and communion rails. The 15th century font has the arms of England, the Swinburne lords of the manor and the de Veres.

The nave walls bear paintings more than seven centuries old including Nativity scenes with the three Magi being warned by an angel as they lie tucked up in their bed; St. Francis preaching to the birds; a pair of gossiping women with attendant demons, and the miraculous restoration to life by St. Nicholas of three lads killed in a pickling barrel by a butcher.

The de Vere arms are also on the font at Bures where rests the wooden figure of a cross-legged knight, and, a mile away in the little thatched Chapel of St. Stephen, which was built in 1218, three martial effigies of earls of that line, removed from Earls Colne Priory, lie upon table tombs on the site of the Christmas Day coronation

LEFT – St. Mary's Church, Wissington.

of the young Edmund of East Anglia. Another chapel of similar date, also lit by lancet windows and dedicated to St. James, is at Lindsey. Close by are the remains of an earlier Norman motte and bailey castle within a curve of the stream which flows on to give Kersey its watersplash at the bottom of a hill from which its old parish church surveys the village once renowned for its weavers.

Across the Stour the restored church at Mount Bures, which stands close by the motte of a Norman castle, has a tower above the crossing and Roman materials in the fabric. Downstream on the Essex side, Wormingford has Norman work in the tower and nave and at Little Horkesley the effigies and brasses of long-dead knights were rescued from the bomb destruction of 1940 to lie in the village's rebuilt church. One of the oak effigies of 13th century mailed knights holds his heart in his hands and there are the brasses of Sir Robert Swynborne and his son, Sir Thomas. A later brass shows Dame Bridget Marney dressed in cloak and gown with her head in a Tudor dog kennel headdress resting upon a cushion.

One of the earliest English memorial brasses is that at Acton of Sir Robert de Bures wearing mail from head to foot. Also in the church is a contrasting memorial to Robert Jennens, a soldier in Marlborough's campaigns, who is seen reclining with his head propped by one hand and his sorrowing wife at his feet. At Lavenham where the Spring family of rich clothiers combined with the 13th Earl of Oxford to build one of Suffolk's noblest churches, the star emblem of the aristocratic patron abounds. Maria Marten, the victim of the celebrated Red Barn murder, is buried at Polstead where the church has Norman arcades with brick arches and Suffolk's only medieval stone spire.

Nayland has a treasured altar painting by Constable of Christ blessing bread and wine and in the medieval splendour of Stoke by Nayland's church are the figures of Sir Francis Mannock looking much like Charles I; Lady Ann Windsor in black farthingale and Sir William Tendring. His daughter conveyed his estates by marriage to the Howards who rose to be scheming Dukes of Norfolk. Among all these reminders of warriors and wars of the past, Boxford has two memorials of more pacific style – the brass of young David Birde asleep in his little bed with shoes beneath, and a tablet to Elizabeth Hyam who was hastened to her end *by a fall that brought on a mortification* in her 113th year.

Where the palmers throng again

Little Walsingham has put its days of *wrackes and bitter woes* behind it. Again the palmers throng in thousands to England's Nazareth. Not that the modern shrine can match the golden, glittering tower tops whose levelling to the ground was bewailed in verse by Philip Howard, the Elizabethan Earl of Arundel.

There have been other and more recent changes, too, along the Walsingham Way since the shrine was reborn in the 1930s. The old railway station wears a 'golden' dome and bell turret and is an Orthodox church dedicated to a forest-dwelling Russian monk (at Great Walsingham the Methodist chapel is now the 'Russian Orthodox Church of the Holy Transfiguration'). Where people waited for trains during the golden age of steam there are icons of archangels and saints. No more do belching locomotives pull rattling carriages of holidaymakers along the line to Wells, passing the restored 'Slipper Chapel' at Houghton St. Giles along the way. There the little 14th century chapel from whence, it is said, medieval pilgrims walked the last stage of the journey barefooted, now has a modern complex of Roman Catholic buildings for company.

The original shrine of Our Lady of Walsingham was established by Richeldis de Faverches, the 11th century lady of the manor, who was instructed in a vision to build a replica of the Holy House of Nazareth. A spring broke forth to mark the site and, as the fame of shrine and its figure of the Madonna became renowned throughout the land, they were enclosed in a chapel administered by monks from the priory founded by Geoffrey de Faverches. Kings and queens journeyed to Walsingham where miracles were claimed and holy relics were stored. But all was swept away at the Reformation by Henry VIII who is said to have walked to the shrine as an unshod pilgrim from East Barsham Manor. The figure of Our Lady of Walsingham was taken to London and put on a bonfire.

Oules do scrike where the sweetest himnes
Lately were songe,
Toades and serpents hold their dennes
Where the palmers did throng.
Weepe, weepe O Walsingham

LEFT – St. Seraphim's Orthodox Church, Lt. Walsingham.

Whose dayes are nightes,
Blessings turned to blasphemies,
Holy deeds to dispites.

Of the Augustinian priory little more than the gatehouse and stark window arch of the eastern wall of the church remain. The Greyfriars' friary, founded just before the Black Death, is also a ruin. Now a new effigy is venerated in the brick and porticoed Anglican Shrine of Our Lady of Walsingham. Also in the village of narrow streets, which converge at a Tudor conduit in Common Place, are modern religious communities, a Methodist Chapel with pyramid roof of 1793 and the parish church of St. Mary, restored to pristine state after a fire in 1961. Saved and restored were the figures of Sir Henry Sydney, cousin of a more famous Elizabethan poet, and his wife Jane, who died in 1638 *after a peregrination of 73 yeares*.

Along the Stiffkey valley are other old and 'holy' places. Little Snoring's church has a detached pre-Conquest tower which is a relic of an earlier church. Inside are a decorated Norman font, a scoreboard of R.A.F. battles and a rarity among Royal Arms – those of James II. In East Barsham church, which has lost chancel and transepts and all but the base stage of its tower which serves as porch, the shrouded figure of Mary Calthorpe is seen arising from her grave.

Further downstream, past the circular ditch and bank ramparts of an Iceni fortress, Warham All Saints church has lost its tower and most of its aisles while at the other end of the village, St. Mary's is redolent with the atmosphere of a Georgian country parish church.

Across the fields from Binham, where the nave of the priory church was saved for parish use, is the little 13th century parish church of Cockthorpe, in which two knights of the sea, John Narbrough and Cloudesley Shovel, were baptised. When Narbrough died at sea Shovel married his widow, rose to high naval rank but was murdered for the rings on his fingers when he was washed ashore after being shipwrecked off the Scillies in 1707. A memorial tells how Dame Barbara Calthorpe was much comforted to see 193 of her children and their offspring as she neared her end in 1639. The little river runs into the sea at Stiffkey where a ledger tells of a thrice wed daughter of a London merchant, Elizabeth Armiger, whose first spouse was a Doctor of Physick by the name of Ahasueres Regemorter!

Blythburgh's trials and seven sinners

Sitting silently on an old bench in Blythburgh church (perchance next to shamed Master Drunkenness whose feet are anchored firmly in the stocks, or tight-fisted Master Avarice perched upon his treasure chest, or belly-holding Master Gluttony) it is not easy to conjure up pictures in the mind of this place's past. In the wide, long, bright silence of the nave beneath huge, motionless wooden angels can the imagination envisage the night the body of a battle-slain king was buried here; the wordly market bustle of sailors and shipwrights, monks and housewives; that terrifying summer Sunday of thunder and lightning when the steeple came crashing through the roof; or Victorian congregations huddling beneath rain-dripping umbrellas?

Upstanding above river and creek, Holy Trinity's gleaming flints and glass seize attention. Retaining only the tower of an earlier building, the Augustinian canons of Blythburgh Priory encouraged the creation of a new church in the 15th century. The unbroken nave-to-chancel roof has wide-winged painted angels lit by 36 clerestory windows; in one of the broad-windowed aisles is the chantry of benefactor Sir John Hopton; and the south porch has an external stoup.

On the nave benches are the celebrated figures of the Seven Deadly Sins – Hypocrisy praying with his eyes open, Sloth still abed, Pride in flowing finery and slit-tongued Slander – as well as other figures representing seasonal labours. The chancel stalls have carved frontals (right) depicting saints, Apostles and, it is claimed, abbess Etheldreda of Ely and her father, Anna, the early Christian king of East Anglia who was buried here in 654 after a battle with Penda and his pagan Mercians. Blythburgh's bearded Jack o' the Clock is late 17th century (nearby Southwold's is two centuries older).

Blythburgh's prosperity, generated by its old market, river-borne trade and shipbuilding, was slipping away even as they built the new church. The larger-hulled ships were unable to reach the town's quays so traders and shipwrights deserted the banks of the Blyth. Unhappy times lay ahead. The Priory was closed and its buildings left to crumble. Then came the great storm of August 1577 when the steeple tumbled and, into the midst of the congregation, so the story goes, burst the devil in the form of a black dog which killed a man and boy before departing to inflict similar destruction and terror on the people of Bungay. Scorch marks on the north door of Blythburgh's church are cited as 'evidence' of the hellish intruder's hasty exit.

In 1643 came William Dowsing on his Parliamentary mission of destruction. At Blythburgh, as elsewhere in the county, he and his men smashed the medieval glass and tore the brass memorial figures and inscriptions from tombs. Iron rings in the pillars near the font are said to be where these desecrators tethered their horses. By 1847, when George Whincop, parish blacksmith for upwards of 50 years, was *By Earth conceal'd, by wood confin'd, And to my native dust consign'd* in the churchyard, the parish church was 'mouldering into ruin' and that was when prudent souls took an umbrella to church when rain clouds threatened. Towards the end of the 19th century the building was closed as unsafe until restoration came to the rescue. Now, happily, those floating angels and figures of human sin need fear no watery downpour from the heavens.

LEFT – Holy Trinity, Blythburgh, and river.

Walstan – Norfolk's own muddy saint

Upstream of Norwich, in the valleys of the Wensum and the Yare, the land is green and gentle – villages have an air of unhurried contentment; a sufficiency of trees line the lanes and climb the lenient contours; and a liberal scatter of churches are set in calm seclusion.

To this niche of Norfolk a thousand years ago, it is said, came Walstan who is dismissively catalogued in one old book as 'saint, guardian of the British peasantry, died 1016'. Such a claim would have raised more than a few sun-burnished hackles hereabout when the Plantagenet Edwards were kings; guardian of the *British* peasantry indeed! Walstan was a singularly Norfolk saint and Bawburgh was his shrine.

The little church, brick-buttressed on its north side as though to stop it toppling down the hill towards the river, has a late Saxon round tower with a conical cap of tiles. The popularity of Walstan's tale generated cash from the pilgrim trade to such a degree that a shrine chapel was built in the 14th century where six chantry priests invoked the saint's blessing on farmers and their beasts of the fields. The Reformation scornfully swept away the Walstan cultus; the shrine was torn down; his hallowed bones were burned and scattered, and slow dilapidation ensued. Two of Bawburgh's priests who did not live to witness such profanity are remembered in chancel brasses. Thomas Tyard, who died in 1505, is shown enshrouded ready for the grave, and William Rechers is commemorated by a chalice. Close by is another shrouded cleric who died in the year Charles II regained his father's throne and Cromwell's Commonwealth was consigned to memory.

The nave, cottage-roofed with warm, red pantiles and mellow brick-stepped gables, was renovated in the early 17th century and the arch to Walstan's shrine survives. But the memory of Walstan toiling in the fields (surely he was a more congenial character than those pious, bossy, royal Saxon women of Ely) has not been totally obliterated. He is shown still on five Norfolk church screen panels, notably at nearby Barnham Broom, Ludham, and, with both his 'trade-marks' of scythe and oxen, at Sparham.

Walstan's cult was proletarian – monarchs who had never got mud in their boots while following plough and oxen, or caloused hands from swinging a harvest scythe, went to Walsingham or Bromholm. Bawburgh's Christian exemplar had ploughed and sown, reaped and mown, and that was why his shrine attracted the oblations of the 'peasantry' whose lives were ruled by the seasons. Walstan, it was claimed, had royal parents – such idealistic dedication had to be the result of aristocratic breeding! – and his mother, Blida, also achieved sainthood plus a dedicatory chapel at Martham.

Walstan's uncomplicated and earthy tale is simply told. Renouncing a life of privilege, he engaged in toil and self-denying poverty as a farm labourer at Taverham. His employers were so pleased by his conduct that they suggested he become their heir. He refused and asked only for the offspring of a cow heavy with calf. Two calves were born and Walstan nurtured them until, one day in the fields, a visitation by angels warned him that his hour of death was near. He died at prayer when he was about 50 years old and his body was placed on a cart hitched to his two oxen. The makeshift hearse crossed over the waters of the Wensum and a series of springs burst forth to mark the journey to Bawburgh.

A sin of which Walstan was guiltless – gossip – was depicted long ago by painters (male ones no doubt) as pairs of chatterbox women on the walls of nearby Colton and Little Melton churches. At Barnham Broom (once called Barnham Ryskes because of the river rushes until yellow broom changed the scene) there is a notable screen with those two East Anglian sister saints, Etheldreda of Ely and Withburga of Dereham with her doe. Taverham church, dedicated to St. Edmund, has a Norman tower and a font with figures including one of its patron saint. Tucked into a corner of East Tuddenham church is the effigy of a knight holding his heart in his hands of the time of Edward I's wars of conquest in Wales.

Colney church has a chalice brass and, over the porch, are cautionary words for drivers set up long before the motorcar age. John Fox died nearby when he was trampled by wagon horses in 1806 – *Tho his Life was humble yet it was deserving of imitation. He was a worthy & useful Member of Society, an honest & industrious Labourer. READER If thou drivest a team be careful & endanger not the Life of another or thine own* – Walstanite virtues indeed!

LEFT – Church of St. Mary and St. Walstan, Bawburgh.

Bowmen and scholars by the Cam

Motorway traffic rushes north-south between London and Cambridge and for a few miles, as it approaches the famed University city, the road runs parallel to the unhasty flowing Cam. Within that elongated, mile-wide 'island' between road and river the 'ford' villages go peacefully about their business.

Long ago, travellers of the Icknield Way came to Little Shelford, Ickleton, Duxford, and Whittlesford to cross the river on their way between fen and forest into Norfolk. To bar this ancient highway against invaders, Celtic tribesmen built a fortress at Wandlebury and, centuries later, the Wuffinga kings of East Anglia raised miles of ramparts and ditches along their vulnerable border against the aggressive pagan warriors of Mercia.

Whittlesford had a church when its lord of the manor, Gyrth Godwinson, died in battle with his king-brother at Hastings in 1066. The nave is Norman work as is the central tower which has two strange figures in the south face stonework beneath the clock – a four-legged, human-headed creature is breathing down the neck of a pouting-lipped, reclining, naked female. These heathen intruders look out across a churchyard shaded by copper beech and horse chestnut wherein past parishioners share the consecrated earth with servicemen from many lands – Australian, Canadian, South African, Czech and Pole – as well as R.A.F. fliers killed in accidents.

The old timber porch, weathered by six centuries of summer sun and winter frost, introduces benefactor Henry Ciprian. His name is on the timbers and he is shown in a red cloak holding a model of the church he enlarged in the Victorian stained glass. Standing beside him is a green-hooded Whittlesford longbowman, a veteran of the Battle of Crecy, with arrows thrust into his belt. A graffiti artist of long ago scratched another bowman into the stone of one of the pillars. An admirer of good bowmanship was Roger Ascham, scholar and tutor of Edward VI and his half-sister, Elizabeth. Ascham, whose son was baptised at Whittlesford's font, wrote about the sport, commending it as a healthier and more moral pastime for the young than cards.

Another advocate of learning was grocer Will Westley. His memorial records that he was *in his Life time an encourager of ye Charity Schools in Cambridge and seeing ye good effects of that most excellent charity* he founded one in his native village *out of a pious design to have ye Children of ye Poor educated in ye fear of God and instructed in ye principles of ye Christian Religion.* This examplary memorial concludes by urging the reader *to go and do likewise.* Sadly for Will Westley, who died in 1723 when he was 38, none of his own eight children, of which three were named after him, had the opportunity to learn much – they all died in infancy.

In the early years of the 20th century Whittlesford's old church found another benefactor at a time of need. He was Henry Gage Spicer, Nonconformist business-man of the nearby paper mills at Sawston. The church was renovated thanks to his generous donation made *in good will to the Church of England and as evidence of a great desire for the reunion of the Christian Churches.* Another mill owner – the village had three mills in Gyrth Godwinson's days – is commemorated by a bulbous urn on the edge of the churchyard. Ebenezer Hollick, who died in 1828, was a Baptist which is why his monument stands in a walled appendage to Whittlesford's quiet God's acre.

Hard by the Cam are the churches of the other ford villages, some with substantial Norman work in their fabric. Ickleton's church incorporates the stonework of previous conquerors, some of the nave arcade columns being of Roman manufacture. A fire in 1979 revealed a wealth of medieval wall paintings and upon a bench is a carving of the archangel Michael weighing souls. There are two old churches at Duxford, each with Norman towers – St. Peter's at the west end, St. John's at the crossing – and chancel lancet windows. A mile downstream is the chapel of St. John's Hospital where medieval wayfarers found rest and shelter.

The Shelfords and their churches are separated by the river which has passed the secluded King's watermill. Both churches have brasses of 15th century priests and at Little Shelford is the cross-legged tomb effigy of the Angevin knight, John de Freville, whose Norman-French inscription tells that he was *seigniour de ceste vile.* As the two Rivers Cam approach their junction Hauxton's old church stands by the village street. It has Norman chancel and nave to which a 15th century tower was added. Within a niche is a 13th century painting of Thomas Becket in mitre and pallium with one hand holding a crosier and the other raised in blessing.

LEFT – Church of St. Mary and St. Andrew, Whittlesford.

'Noe strains of Art to speake thy woorth'

Monastery and market, church and castle – the medieval symbols of wealth and power – were once all grouped east of the Cam at Saffron Walden where tributaries of that river formed a star-shaped indent among the low hills. Walden Abbey has gone, superseded by a mansion bearing the name of a Lord Chancellor of whom Thomas Fuller, historian and theologian, said his heart was as black and hard as the slate of his tomb in the town's parish church. The castle, built by the Mandevilles who founded the monastery, is a ruin.

Forgive me worthy freind that I presume
To offer low incomiums on thy tombe.
Had I the mighty Cowley soule one hower,
His flight of witt and his Seraphick power,
I'd doe thee right in such a hight of words
Should out live time and all his dull Records.
But hold, there needs noe strains of Art
To speake thy woorth . . . so begins an epitaph on one of the old ledgers which still pave the church floor. With the Jacobean mansion of Audley End, one of the largest and finest churches in the county, Tudor inns, oversailing homes from the days of the cloth trade, Georgian houses and a wide common with a maze, Saffron Walden has much of its own to speak its worth.

Such was the prosperity engendered by the cloth trade and the growing of the saffron crocus to provide a yellow dye (the first bulb was smuggled back to England hidden in a pilgrim's staff so the story goes) that the town's name was changed and they carved the crocus into the roof when they rebuilt the church. This imposing building with tower and 19th century stone spire rising almost 200 feet towards the sky, aisles as wide as the nave and the sweep of tall arcades, was raised over some eighty years after a destructive storm in 1445.

Thomas Audley was Sir Thomas More's successor as Lord Chancellor of England and he presided over the Court of Augmentations which disposed of monastic estates at the dissolution of the monasteries by Henry VIII. Audley's loyal service to the tyrant king was rewarded by his acquisition of Walden Abbey and the town's castle. Shortly before *the stroke of death's inevitable dart* in 1544, Lord Audley founded Magdalene College,

LEFT – St. Mary's Church, Wendens Ambo.

Cambridge, in a hostel for student monks. Through his daughter, who married the Duke of Norfolk, Audley's Walden estate came to Thomas Howard, Earl of Suffolk, who built a vast and costly mansion using cash he had embezzled from his high office. Shrewd James I commented that it was too big for a king but sufficient for a Lord Treasurer! In later years Charles II used it as a palace, found it too expensive and returned it to the Howards who pulled down much of it. In the 18th century Robert Adam directed its restoration and the park was landscaped by 'Capability' Brown.

Hempstead, birthplace of highwayman Dick Turpin, has Tudor brasses in its 14th century church and memorials to the Harvey family including a bust of doctor William Harvey, discoverer of the circulation of the blood and sufferer from gout which he treated by sitting outdoors in frosty weather with his feet in water until, numb with cold, he hurried to warm himself by the fire. Radwinter's rector, William Harrison, whose household consumed 200 gallons of home-brewed beer a month, conducted services with blue ice in the church during the cold Elizabethan winters and tended 300 different plants in his garden in summer as well as writing his books. His church was much rebuilt in the 19th century when it gained a tower and Wimbish's church of Norman date had its tower demolished.

West of the Cam Strethall's isolated church has a Saxon nave and at Wendens Ambo there are Roman bricks around one doorway and a Norman tower topped by a Hertfordshire spike. The approach to the church serving the two parishes which were united when Charles II restored the monarchy is a delight. On one side are cottages fronted by hollyhocks, on the other a huge old thatched barn. The bust of a Charles II 'lookalike', John Withers, is in the church tower at Arkesden, an attractive village of many thatched cottages beside the Wicken Water. Lying on a six-poster tomb are Richard Cutte and his wife Mary, she the daughter of a king's chief butler. Beneath are the named figures of their children in primogenitive order of precedence, but all the sons have been beheaded (those Cromwellians who turned Walden's church into an eating hall are blamed). With words which tell of the lineage of this pair of Tudor worthies whose clay rests in this cold mansion is a familiar caution – *As ye nowe are, so once weare we; as we nowe are, so shall ye be.*

Juggernauts and 'calm, refulgent groves'

Loaded juggernauts bound for Birmingham or Brussels, Manchester or Munich, Wolverhampton or wherever, slice through Suffolk in an hour, courtesy of the A45. On either side, unheeded by those in such unhindered haste, are fields and farms, hills and woods not yet anonymously numbered but bearing the names they acquired long ago in vanished lifetimes.

There are warrens and groves aplenty; Abbey, Rectory and Holyoak farms; Chapel and Devil's hills; Gallows fields and Tinkers wood; Packway, Stoney, Kiln and Cripples lanes and a Lady's Well. Here, east of Bury St. Edmunds, are old churches whose names, like the stone of their walls and the wood of their furnishings, reflect the differing ages of their construction.

Near a red brick hall and barns, a field track from a lane leads to a tiny reed-thatched church whose uncommon dedication hints at its age – St Augustine's, Harleston. The hum of distant hurrying drifts across the fields to the little towerless church with Norman nave and door, lancet windows and weatherboarded Victorian bell turret. The scrupulously burnished interior has a 14th century screen, plain benches, and, for mid-winter evensong, the necessary paraffin lamps bracketed to the walls, candle holders on the choir stalls and an old candlestick on the pulpit. There is no electricity except for the car battery attached to the little 'Angelus Organ'. In the churchyard where, as one headstone puts it, *suffring mortal, all thy trials are o'er* and *the last great debt of nature is repaid*, five rusting iron grave markers tell of a family's five children who died one after the other in little more than a month. Hopefully, as another headstone couplet says, eas'd of their load their gentle spirits rove *through calm, refulgent and celestial groves*.

Westward along the lane is another towerless building of even rarer dedication. Shelland's formerly donative Gothic chapel of King Charles the Martyr was rebuilt and refurnished in 1767. In the nave of yellow brick floor and red rafters, box pews cluster around the three-decker pulpit and old benches flank the 36-tune barrel organ.

Woolpit's church of St. Mary – by far the most popular East Anglian medieval patron saint – has a dominating

LEFT – St. Augstine's Church, Harleston.

tower and spire with the message * Glory to God * in the highest * on earth peace * good will to men* upon its faces below flying buttresses and parapet. This Victorian pointer was no guide to pilgrims seeking the parish's Lady's Well whose waters were said to be good for the eyes. The earthly glories of the church are in its medieval craftsmanship of the porch stonework and the woodwork of its roof and benches (below).

There are more carved roof figures and bench-end beasts at Wetherden. Like Woolpit, this St. Mary's suffered the attention of window-smasher William Dowsing who also hacked at the tomb inscription of Sir John Sulyard where it sought God's mercy upon his soul. The arms of Chief Justice and benefactor, Sir John Sulyard, appear in the woodwork of the aisle he built wherein is his monument. Haughley's St. Mary's has the first stage of the tower as its south porch where they used to hang leather fire buckets dated 1725 and 1757. The old font is guarded by quartets of lions and wild men and adjoining the churchyard is the Norman moated motte and bailey castle which was stormed by Flemish mercenaries in 1173 before they were scattered by knights as they tried to bypass Bury St. Edmunds. Elmswell's church has a younger neighbour of thoroughly unmartial intent; a row of almshouses for *six poore women widows* built in 1614 by another judge, Sir Robert Gardener, *sometime Lord of these manors of Elmswell & Wolpit*. His effigy is in the church with one of nature's juggernauts, a rhinoceros, at his feet.

Cambridge – 'and then the heaven espy'

There are many images of Cambridge – medieval and modern; seasonal and parvenu; flashy, tawdry, romantic; even divine. The riverside market town where the Norman Conqueror had built a castle became a dichotomous, often pestilential, sometimes riotous community wherein the learned and the labourer were forced into necessary co-existence. Enriched by kings, queens, bishops and nobles, the enclave of colleges, scholarship and disputation became the epicentre of the English Reformation.

The University suffered much during the pendulum swings of religious dominance until the inevitable 18th century reaction brought a soporific stagnancy interrupted by occasional genius. Change was forced upon the University in the 19th century – the curriculum was broadened, new colleges founded (some for women), Fellows permitted to marry and the much resented University's licensing powers ended.

Medieval Cambridge had many religious buildings within its small area. There were 13 churches, including the 12th century circular Holy Sepulchre; conventual buildings, some later transformed into colleges (Jesus College was a nunnery, Magdalene a monks' hostel and Sidney Sussex was built on the site of a Franciscan house), and, as time went on, the colleges were allowed their own chapels. For decades St. Mary the Great was at the hub of university life – scene of disputations, recantations, University sermons, and, until the building of the Senate House in 1730, degree award ceremonies. The early colleges used the Cambridge churches for worship; Peterhouse, Cambridge's oldest college, founded by Bishop of Ely, Hugh de Balsham, in 1284, was linked by a gallery of St. Mary the Less while Corpus Christi, established by the town's religious guilds, was connected to St. Bene't's, a Saxon church and the oldest building in the county.

King's College Chapel – *this immense and glorious Work of fine intelligence* was how Wordsworth (a student at St. John's) described it – was built at the command of kings. Started by Henry VI in 1446, its construction was interrupted by the Wars of the Roses until it was completed a century later by Henry VIII. Its spectacular fan-vaulting, woodwork and great windows of 16th century glass make it one of the great, late medieval buildings of Europe. Tudor emblems abound – dragons, roses, greyhounds and the Beaufort portcullis. Lady Margaret Beaufort, Henry VIII's grandmother, had created St. John's College and refounded Christ's from its predecessor, God's House, which had had to move to make way for King's.

As the chapel neared completion radical religious ideas were taking root. During the final years of Henry's life, and more so during the reign of Edward VI, Protestantism flourished. Martin Bucer, a German theologian, joined Cranmer, Latimer and Ridley in preaching in Cambridge. University and town were pushed into the vanguard of the Reformation. Queen Mary attempted to restore Catholicism; she expelled Protestants from the colleges; Cranmer, Latimer and Ridley, all educated at Cambridge, were burned in the fires of persecution, and even Bucer's bones were dug up and burned in the market place. In Elizabeth's reign Catholics were purged and persecuted; during the Civil War Royalist college Masters and Fellows were ejected and at the Restoration it was the Puritans who were expelled. It would be another two centuries before religious bars to student admissions were abolished.

Henry VIII had also founded Cambridge's largest college, Trinity, whose chapel was begun in daughter Mary's reign. The ante-chapel is a Valhalla of the great – statues of Newton, Francis Bacon, Tennyson, Macaulay, Barrow, and Whewell; busts of others and more than 100 brass wall plates. Pembroke College, the first to be allowed its own chapel, now has a chapel given by Matthew Wren, Bishop of Ely, who spent 18 years in the Tower of London during the Cromwellian years. It was the first building completed by his nephew, Christopher, and with the portraits of college benefactors in the windows are pictures of Denny Abbey, Ely Cathedral, Soham Church and Framlingham Castle. Across the road at 'Little St. Mary', with its stars and stripes memorial (the origin of 'Old Glory'?) to the Rev. Godfrey Washington, the glass doors are engraved with words by George Herbert, poet and Fellow of Trinity –

A man that looks on glass,
On it may stay his eye,
Or, if he pleaseth, through it pass,
And then the heaven espy.

LEFT – King's College Chapel, Cambridge.

Island of bluebells, Bromholm and angels

Only a mile from the gas terminal at Bacton, where 20th century technology allows Man to suck out the fuel from beneath the shrouding waters of the North Sea, is an undisturbed spot where, if you've a mind to let it, time can stand still. From the hamlet of Edingthorpe, a narrow lane becomes a field-flanked track which climbs up the hill to a meadowy, island churchyard guarded by a curtain of trees, where, come May, the grass is speckled with bluebells.

The round, tapering Norman tower topped by octagonal belfry; thatched nave with windows of diverse design; pantiled chancel and porch; doorways built when Lionhearted Richard I neglected his realm to go Crusading – all these betray the building's old and piecemeal evolution. Inside there is bright but utilitarian rusticity with an old St. Christopher wall painting to comfort any apprehensive traveller or brooding parishioner resting on the yeoman benches below.

Above the rood loft stairs is a niche with painted border, and in the mix of woodwork is a 14th century screen with picture panels of saints, a Tudor reading desk and Stuart pulpit. Among the six saints on the screen is James the Great with his pilgrim staff and scallop shell, the 'badge' of his Spanish shrine at Compostella. Here, where the wind blows in from the North Sea, the lychgate is a memorial to a soldier of the Norfolk Regiment who endured the early First World War battles in France but whose grave was the warmer waters of the Aegean when his troopship was sunk in 1915.

In centuries past men and women leaning on pilgrim staves passed by Edingthorpe on their way to a shrine famed for its possession of a prized relic – the Holy Roode of Bromholm. The little priory had been founded at Bacton in 1113 but it would never have achieved mention in the lines of Chaucer or Langland's 'Vision of Piers the Plowman' but for its claim to have acquired part of the True Cross from a wandering, refugee monk whose piece of old wood had been rejected as fraudulent by richer monastic houses. Now only ruins mark the spot where miracle cures were said to have occurred and where John Paston's body was laid to rest in 1466 amid

LEFT – All Saints' Church, Edingthorpe.

the flicker of torchlight (the window glass had to be removed to let out the overpowering smoke) and feasting in 1466. The menu included 90 pigs and calves and many gallons of beer and wine.

In the Pastons' home village, the thatched church has several memorials to that famous family and stands near their huge, old, flinten barn. The letters written by the Pastons give a vivid picture of 15th century life and their private and political tribulations, including the month-long siege and surrender of their castle at Caister to 3,000 men led by Thomas Mowbray, Duke of Norfolk, in 1469. In Paston church is a giant St. Christopher and the alabaster figure of Dame Katherine Paston who died in 1629, for which sculptor Nicholas Stone was paid the then huge sum of £340.

Along the littoral between Cromer and Happisburgh old churches plenteously dot the landscape, each one but a mile or so from its nearest neighbour. At Trunch the great and rare treasure is the intricately carved font canopy (one of only four in England) raised high on six legs, with more fine carving in roof, stalls and screen. Knapton's pride is its roof, a masterpiece testifying to the skill of Tudor carpenters. Gazing down from the double hammerbeam construction built in 1504 by the rector, John Smithe, are tiers of angels, 138 in number, some bearing scrolls or shields and some playing musical instruments. The font cover bears a Greek inscription which reads the same both ways – *Wash my sins and not my face only.*

Walcott's 15th century church stands back from its village and holiday homes and has sedilia and piscina beneath decorated arches and a ledger to a 17th century priest with its incised words in a variety of languages. The tall tower of Happisburgh church is, like the red and white banded lighthouse at the other end of the village, an imposing landmark for shipping. Carved upon the font which was new when most of the church was rebuilt during the 15th century, are angel musicians, lions and wildmen. In the churchyard lie many victims of past tragedies when sea and wind combined in displays of frightening fury. An example of the sea's control along the shifting Norfolk coastline is the now churchless parish of Eccles. Twice the village has lost old churches to the stormy waves and for years only the tower remained protruding from the sand dunes.

Glossary of terms often found in church guides.

Abacus – stone slab on the top of a column.

Abbey – community of monks or nuns under the jurisdiction of an abbot or abbess.

Aisle – outwards extension parallel to the north or south of the nave and chancel. The arches separating nave and aisle usually mark line of the original exterior nave wall. From the Latin for wing.

Alms box – container for donations. Bramford's is below the words 'Remember ye pore. The scripture doth record What to them is geven is lent unto the Lord 1591'.

Apse – rounded or polygonal end to chancel or extension of transept.

Arcade – line of arches (as demark nave and aisle). Blind arcade – a series of blocked arches incorporated into wall for decoration or extra strength as on the exterior of Norman tower at South Lopham.

Architectural periods – the dating of medieval churches relies heavily upon recognition of the architectural style of the construction. The periods have their individual characteristics. There were, however, overlaps of several years at beginning and ending of periods, styles did not change 'overnight'. The earliest in extant buildings is the **Saxon** period from the 7th century to the Norman Conquest of 1066. The **Norman** period (also known as Romanesque) of 1066 to the late 12th century was a period of much ecclesiastical building. The English **Gothic** period is subdivided into – **Early English**, late 12th century – 1300; **Decorated** late 13th century to 1350 (the Black Death) and then **Perpendicular** which was the predominant style from 1350 until the **Classical** style of the 17th century.

Ashlar – square blocks of stone for exterior facing.

Aumbry – wall cupboard, usually near altar, for ritual vessels.

Belfry – originally a tower strongroom where valuables were stored. Now the room containing the bells.

Bench – long seat, usually of wood with back-rest, sometimes with carving of figures and grotesque animals. Notable examples at Athelington, Bressingham, Dennington, Fressingfield, Wiggenhall St Mary the Virgin, and Wiggenhall St Germans.

Bequest board – painted notice board detailing local charity or benefaction, usually found in tower.

Box pew – enclosed bench seating entered by a door. Examples at Shelland, Thurning, Worstead.

Campanile – detached bell-tower as at West Walton, Beccles. At East Bergholt the tower is unfinished so the bells are in a timber cage in the churchyard.

Canopy of honour – also celure, decorated roof area usually above rood at east (chancel) end of nave.

Capital – top of a column.

Cartouche – scroll shaped wall tablet.

Chancel – eastern section of church containing the altar, from Latin word for screen which separated it from the main body.

Chantry – chapel often in aisle where masses were said for souls of wealthy benefactors. Clopton chapel, Long Melford is a fine example.

Charnel House – depository of bones.

Chest – many churches have old wooden, sometimes iron bound, chests in which parish documents and valuables were stored. One of the oldest in the region is at Hindringham.

Choir – that part of church, usually in chancel, occupied by clergy and choristers.

Clerestory – upper section of nave walls above aisle roof level with inserted windows to give extra light.

Consecration cross – painted or incised cross on wall performed at dedication of the building.

Corbel – stone or timber projecting from wall to support roof beam or arch.

Crossing – area of intersection of chancel, nave and transepts, usually below a central tower.

Crypt – 'hidden' chamber or vault often beneath chancel; in churches burial place of local gentry; in cathedrals an underground chapel.

Decalogue – also commandment boards, usually wall mounted boards of the Ten Commandments, Lord's Prayer and Creed; some with paintings of Moses and Aaron as at Redgrave and Gt. Snoring.

Diaper – decorative pattern on walls, sometimes formed by using bricks of different colour.

Doom – depiction of Judgement Day; example at Wenhaston.

Easter Sepulchre – decorated recess in chancel wall where the Host and crucifix were symbolically placed from Good Friday to Easter Day. Examples are at Blythburgh, Baconsthorpe and Cockfield.

Flushwork – decorative stone and flint patterns, notable feature of many East Anglian churches. Examples at Gipping and Long Melford.

Font – bowl for holding water for important Christian sacrament of baptism. Many styles can be seen in East Anglia. Historically notable is the Norman font at Burnham Deepdale with 12 seasonal pictures such as threshing, killing a pig and a Christmas feast. Seven sacrament fonts depicting baptism, confirmation, extreme unction, mass, matrimony, ordination and penance are almost exclusively East Anglian. Examples are at Cratfield, Sloley and Laxfield. Notable examples of font covers are at Castle Acre, North Walsham and Ufford; canopy at Trunch.

Fresco – mural painting made before the plaster dried.

Friary – a convent of friars.

Galilee – porch or chapel at western end of church.

Gargoyle – projecting waterspout to throw water away from walls, often grotesquely carved, from Latin for throat.

Hatchment – diamond shaped board showing the arms of deceased person, carried in 18th and 19th century funeral processions then hung in church. They tell sex and marital status of deceased – black background and single arms for bachelor; divided in two for widower; single arms in lozenge for spinster; divided arms in lozenge for widow; divided background of black to left and white to right (as seen) means married man who died before wife; reverse for wife who pre-deceased her husband. Usually hung in church tower. Numerous hatchments of Bacon and Holt families at Redgrave.

Hour glass – large egg timer shaped glass near pulpit used to time sermons. Earl Stonham has a trio of glasses with different amounts of sand to time quarter, half and three-quarters of the hour.

Jack o' the Clock – rare mechanical figure which hits a bell. Can be seen at Blythburgh and Southwold.

Lancet – tall, narrow window, a feature of Early English period.

Lectern – book stand for the Bible, often shaped like an eagle with wings outstretched. Some, as at Clare, have slot in the beak for receiving coins.

Ledger – large, flat stone over a grave, usually in church floor. Some have heraldic arms, laudatory and amusing inscriptions. The tragic tale of Bridgett Applewhaite at Bramfield and the epitaph of a fox-hunting fanatic at Cantley are notable curiosities.

Light – glazed or open sections of windows. Large windows contain numerous 'lights' delineated by mullions.

Long and short – alternating horizontal and vertical stones, a feature of Saxon building.

Lychgate – roofed shelter at entrance to churchyard, from Anglo-Saxon word lych meaning corpse.

Misericord – bracket frequently carved with grotesque on underside of hinged seat to give support when standing.

Mullion – verticals which divide the 'lights' of windows.

Nave – main section of the church west of chancel.

Ogee – curving moulding, concave and convex.

Parclose – screen separating a chapel from rest of the building. Examples at Dennington and Lavenham.

Pilaster – pillar attached to and projecting from a wall.

Piscina – niche basin usually in south wall of chancel where vessels were cleansed, hole (often now blocked) allowed drainage. Double piscinas were introduced so that the priest could wash vessels in one and his hands in another.

Poppyhead – decorative carving on top of bench-ends.

Priest's door – small door usually on chancel south side.

Priory – monastic house under the leadership of a prior of prioress.

Putlog hole – apertures to support medieval scaffolding.

Pulpit – elevated platform for preachers. Vary from 15th century wine glass shape to huge three-deckers.

Quoin – dressed stone used at angle of wall junctions.

Reredos – decorative panel behind the altar.

Retable – decorative carving or painting above the back of an altar. Thornham Parva's is a noted example.

Rood – crucifix; the rood screen delineated nave from chancel and many with panel paintings of saints remain; the **rood lofts**, a gallery above the screen, were destroyed at the Reformation (examples survive at Eye and Attleborough); **rood beam** was the horizontal upon which the rood stood; **rood stairs**, often cut into wall or pillar, gave access to the loft.

Roofs – the skills of medieval builders is displayed in timber roofs which were made without nails or bolts. Examples are: king-post – single upright from the tie-beam to ridge-beam or from tie-beam to collar-beam (a tie-beam high within the roof angle); queenposts – two uprights from tie-beam; hammer-beam – a beam projecting from wall bearing the arch brace, in a double hammer-beam roof the hammer-beams carry two tiers of roof braces. Among East Anglia's finest timber church roofs are those at March, Woolpit, Knapton, Cawston, and Needham Market.

Royal Arms – Carved or painted royal arms ordered to be displayed after the Reformation. Fine carved set (William III) at Shelton; at Tivetshall St. Margaret arms of Elizabeth I appear above the Ten Commandments dated 1587 which Richard Russel and Jaffrye Neve 'in there tyme they caused this for to be done'.

Saltire Cross – diagonal or St. Andrew's cross.

Sanctuary – area around altar, often marked by rails.

Sanctus bell – bell usually housed in a small turret on church roof at junction of nave and chancel which was rung during the mass. Examples of sanctus bell turrets are at Walpole St. Peter and Wiggenhall St. Mary Magdalene.

Scratch dial – exterior south side wall sundial. A series of grooves below hole for gnomen. At Cowlinge it is upside down.

Sedilia – graduated seating with decorated canopies on south side of chancel for priests.

Soffit – underside of an arch, lintel or ceiling.

Spandrel – triangular area between arches or that formed by roof beams and posts.

Squint – (hagioscope) wall hole to allow view of main altar. Examples at Long Melford and Ludham.

Stalls – seating, often decorated, in chancel or choir.

Stoup – Holy water basin near church door or porch.

Tester – or sounding board; canopy above pulpit. Many examples include those at Gislingham, Kedington, Thurning and Worlingworth.

Transept – transverse section of cruciform-plan church.

Triforium – gallery or arcade between nave pier-arches and clerestory.

Tympanum – semicircular space between door lintel and arch above; sculpted decoration varies, Pampisford has a crude arch and figure design; above Prior's Door at Ely Cathedral is an elaborate Christ in Majesty.

Woodwose – long-haired, club-carrying wild man to be seen on font stems (as at Middleton, Orford and Happisburgh) or above porch (Yaxley, Burwell)

Weepers – small effigies on the sides of medieval tombs.

Index of Persons

Index of Places